Suburbs: A Very Short Introduction

VERY SHORT INTRODUCTIONS are for anyone wanting a stimulating and accessible way into a new subject. They are written by experts, and have been translated into more than 45 different languages.

The series began in 1995, and now covers a wide variety of topics in every discipline. The VSI library currently contains over 700 volumes—a Very Short Introduction to everything from Psychology and Philosophy of Science to American History and Relativity—and continues to grow in every subject area.

Very Short Introductions available now:

Available soon:

For more information visit our website

www.oup.com/vsi/

Carl Abbott

SUBURBS

A Very Short Introduction

OXFORD
UNIVERSITY PRESS

OXFORD
UNIVERSITY PRESS

Oxford University Press is a department of the University of Oxford.
It furthers the University's objective of excellence in research, scholarship,
and education by publishing worldwide. Oxford is a registered trade mark of
Oxford University Press in the UK and certain other countries.

Published in the United States of America by Oxford University Press
198 Madison Avenue, New York, NY 10016, United States of America.

Library of Congress Cataloging-in-Publication Data

Names: Abbott, Carl, 1944- author.
Title: Suburbs : a very short introduction / Carl Abbott.
Description: New York, NY : Oxford University Press, [2023] |
Series: Very short introductions | Includes bibliographical references and index.
Identifiers: LCCN 2022037232 | ISBN 9780197599242 (paperback) |
ISBN 9780197599266 (epub)
Subjects: LCSH: Suburbs—History. | Urbanization—History.
Classification: LCC HT351 .A23 2023 | DDC 307.7409—dc23/eng/20220817
LC record available at https://lccn.loc.gov/2022037232

1 3 5 7 9 8 6 4 2

Printed and bound by
CPI Group (UK) Ltd, Croydon, CR0 4YY

Contents

List of illustrations

Acknowledgments

This book has benefited from the direct advice, suggestions, and assistance of Kristin Stapleton, Evguenia Davidova, Ryan Centner, Sonia Hirt, Christian Smigiel, Sohyun Park, and Kyung-Min Kim. I also note the invaluable research and publications of the Global Suburbanisms research collaborative based at York University in Canada, involving dozens of scholars around the world.

Introduction

What is a suburb?

Suburbs are like peanut butter. The world has been urbanizing more and more rapidly for the past 200 years, reaching a global urban population of more than four billion in 2020. Cities with swelling populations have only two options—grow up or grow out. The first choice is to intensify and solidify development within the existing footprint by filling in empty land and erecting taller and taller buildings. The second choice is for extensive development that spreads activity onto land beyond the urban edge. The first is the chocolate sundae approach, sprinkling more and more syrup, nuts, and cherries onto a mound of ice cream. The second is the peanut butter approach, spreading a big glop out toward the edges of a slice of bread. Downtown skyscrapers are the cherries, and suburbs are the peanut butter.

Most of the world is choosing peanut butter (a Chinese term for suburbanization roughly translates to "make a big pancake"). All around the world, cities are consuming land at a faster pace than their population has been increasing, meaning that overall urban population densities are dropping. Development patterns and types in the twenty-first century look different than they did in the nineteenth and even twentieth centuries. This is true for metropolitan Atlanta, for greater Vancouver, and for Paris. It is equally true for Accra, where the population grew by 5.3 percent per year from 1991 to 2014 but the built-up area grew by 7.8 percent.

The world is well into its second century of suburbanization. Residents of the booming industrial cities of Britain and the United States began to move to the urban outskirts in large numbers by the mid-nineteenth century. By the 1950s and 1960s, rural migrants to cities in Eastern Europe, Asia, Africa, and Latin America were settling in massive numbers in new housing that ringed cities from Bucharest to Bogotá. In the twenty-first century, a cul-de-sac neighborhood in Henderson, Nevada, a 1920s council estate outside London, a high-rise new town around Seoul, or the *barriada* Carmen de la Legua outside Lima look different, but they are all parts of a suburban world.

Suburb and *suburbs* are slippery terms that call up clear and shared images for many North Americans, who often draw on the community where they grew up or where they now live. They may think of an iconic television show like *The Brady Bunch* (1969–74), with its opening shot of a house in North Hollywood, California, or the *Adventures of Ozzie and Harriet* (1952–66) and the Nelson family's very real house in Hollywood. Depending on their age, they may remember 211 Pine Street in *Leave It to Beaver* (1957–63) or Wisteria Lane in *Desperate Housewives* (2004–12)— both filmed on the same Colonial Lane set at Universal Studios in Burbank, California. The television shows reference a commonly accepted definition that suburbs are relatively new and largely residential settlements dominated by detached single-family houses.

This common response is really an invocation of *suburbia*, a very special subcategory of peripheral urbanization in English-speaking countries. To speak of suburbia is to emphasize a way of life that suburbs presumably foster, in contrast to an urban way of life. In situation comedies suburbia is where folks chat over the back fence, whether in suburban Detroit in the American television show *Home Improvement* (1991–99) or in suburban London in the British show *The Good Life* (1975–78). Upscale suburbia has a less happy side in films like *Ordinary People,*

The Ice Storm, and *Far from Heaven* that reflect a take on suburbia associated with American writers like John Cheever and John Updike. Suburbia is also where Russian spies in *The Americans* (2013–18) find they can best blend into US society.

Studies of US suburbs that try to bypass the stereotype most often use a quick statistical shortcut. The US Census conveniently defines metropolitan areas as one or more heavily urbanized counties with a large city at the focus. Suburbs are defined by subtraction as inside the metro area but outside the municipal boundaries of the core city. By this measure, there were more suburbanites than either city people or country people by 1970 and more suburbanites than the other two groups put together by 2000.

This rough distinction works reasonably well for social scientists doing comparative analysis across metropolitan regions. In the later twentieth century it usually matched local thinking. Dayton, Ohio, was the city; Kettering and Trotwood were suburbs. Portland, Oregon, was the city; Beaverton and Lake Oswego were suburbs. It is less useful in the third decade of the twenty-first century. One problem is that the Census Bureau repeatedly adds outlying counties that meet its very technical criteria for metropolitan inclusion, even though the residents of Bradford, Ohio, are unlikely to think of any part of their town as a Dayton suburb. The same is true for Carson, Washington, and Portland. Some counties are so large as to make the shorthand look silly—are the mosquitoes of Minnesota's Boundary Waters Canoe Area Wilderness also Duluth suburbanites?

A related problem is that some core cities are small and tightly bounded and others have expansive boundaries. Chicago annexed huge tracts of occupied and unoccupied territory in 1889 and then basically stopped growing, allowing ring after ring of suburban municipalities to grow, but San Antonio kept absorbing outlying territory well into the twenty-first century. The Unified City of

Winnipeg (1972) takes in nearly all peripheral or suburban development, but the core city of Adelaide has only 2 percent of the metropolitan population. Every nation has different traditions, rules, and political balance, making comparisons both challenging and of doubtful value.

An alternative is to devise a functional definition that ignores political boundaries to capture some essential facet of low-density "suburban" development. Canadian researchers used patterns of transit use to divide metropolitan areas into active cores (lots of biking and walking), transit suburbs, automobile suburbs, and exurbs or low-density fringe development. They concluded that two-thirds of all Canadians live in suburbs, to the surprise or even consternation of many compatriots. Australian researchers have found roughly the same proportion. Other experts try to categorize US neighborhoods by the average age of housing—for example, were more housing units in a zip code built before 1980 or after 1980?—or by a combination of economic and demographic factors yielding variously five, six, or ten types. Self-confident journalist David Brooks generalized about lifestyles to distinguish among "crunchy" granola suburbs like Takoma Park, Maryland; "bistroworld" suburbs of comfortable professionals like Bethesda, Maryland; and middle-class cul-de-sac suburbs like much of Fairfax County, Virginia.

Alas, what may be helpful for North America is seldom useful elsewhere. Every nation uses its own census categories and geographies, so statistical approaches work within a country but not for comparisons across national borders. Language also gets in the way, even among English-speaking nations. People in Britain apply *suburb* to individual districts and towns based heavily on social evaluation rather than precise statistics. Australians are generally proud to claim to be the first suburban nation, and they call almost every urban neighborhood a suburb, whether it was developed in the 1910s or 2010s. The mid-sized metropolis of Perth counts more than 350 such suburbs. It is similar in New Zealand, whose Geographic Names Board defines suburb as "an identifiable area within a local authority area, usually urban in character, with facilities such as those for education, transport, and shopping." Examples range from spiffy new subdivisions overlooking Christchurch to picturesque Devonport across the harbor from downtown Auckland. Anglophone Canada uses suburb in much the same way as the United States does. Francophone Quebec does not, taking its terminology from France, where the newer districts that ring historic cities are *les banlieues*. To facilitate international comparisons, Chinese geographers and planners have adopted *jiaoqu* for everything outside Beijing's two inner-city districts but still under jurisdiction of the municipality. India has a variety of terms for different types of peripheral settlements rather than a single inclusive category.

Scholars sometimes try a detour around the language problem by proposing *periurban* to refer to development on the edges or outskirts of urban areas. It avoids the suburbia implications of suburb, and it supposedly encompasses the wide range of peripheral development that is known as *banlieue* in Cambodia and France, as *Stadtrand* in Germany, as *prigorod* in Russia, and as *extrarradio* ("outskirts") in Spanish-speaking countries. However, *periurban* is loved only by academics and a few planning officials and seldom makes its way into everyday language. This book sticks to "suburbs" as the comprehensive term for all types of peripheral urbanization. Suburbs are far more than stereotypical suburbia. In the best and simplest definition offered by the city planner Charles Abrams, a suburb is "a district, usually residential, on the outskirts of a city." Suburbs are all the pockets and rings of newer development on the outskirts of core cities, whether Boston, Buenos Aires, or Beijing.

The urban periphery is in constant change. Older suburbs age, sometimes gracefully and sometimes not. New rural or vacant land is developed for housing and economic activity, only to age in its turn. I have lived most of my life in suburban houses. The two where I lived from birth through high school were built in the 1940s in new subdivisions on the outskirts of Knoxville and Dayton. The new neighborhoods looked suburban. Two other houses where I have lived as an adult were built in the 1920s in what were then new neighborhoods; by the 1970s, when I moved into each in turn, people in Norfolk and Portland considered them marginally troubled urban neighborhoods, but they were suburban at their birth. The key questions are when and where new outlying development has occurred for cities around the world, what sorts of suburban landscapes have emerged, who has used and inhabited those buildings, and how those people and uses have changed.

The outer rings of urban areas have always been diverse in functions and people. As the sociologist William F. Ogburn noted in 1937, suburbs are the natural expansion of the city and display as much variety as the cities they surround. Differences between cities and suburbs are more differences of degree than of kind. Pointing to the Brady Bunch ignores the reality that suburban districts have always been full of poor people, immigrants, working-class families, and people of color. They have also been sites of factories, office buildings, and trash-disposal facilities. Every metropolitan region has a complex suburban geography conditioned by national history, culture, and political choices. There is great diversity among the outlying districts of Detroit and Los Angeles, but also among those of Paris and Budapest and São Paulo.

Suburbs past and present have been places of aspiration. Writing in 1899, the social scientist Adna F. Weber recognized the attraction of new, lower-density neighborhoods for the people of East London slums and New York tenement buildings. He argued that "the 'rise of the suburbs'. . . furnishes the solid basis of a hope that the evils of city life, so far as they result from overcrowding, may be in large part removed." New neighborhoods on the urban edge have long attracted families hoping to announce their social status and other families looking for nothing more than a place to call their own. The new houses, apartments, and neighborhoods may sometimes disappoint, but they continue to be the homes of choice each year for millions of families who are creating a complex and intriguing metropolitan landscape.

Critics sometimes conflate suburbanization with sprawl, but they are not the same. Sprawl is more specific because it refers only to the physical form of peripheral growth. It is also an extremely slippery concept. We tend to apply it to new outlying development that we dislike. We may think that a landscape sprawls because it is ugly and unappealing; because it is inadequately planned and costly to provide with services; because it is scattered, chaotic, and untidy; because it chews up orange groves and berry fields; because it lacks the human scale of a city; or because its auto dependency accelerates global warming. The list can go on. Few observers rhapsodize over "sprawl, beautiful sprawl," even when they defend and advocate suburbanization.

Sprawl is tricky to measure because critics stuff so many problems into a single word. Low-density development by itself is not a good measure, in part because actual density of population or employment varies widely within suburban regions. One effort to define sprawl scores for US metropolitan areas used density, street connectivity, and land use mix to create a single index. There was no surprise when the researchers announced that Riverside, California, and Greensboro, North Carolina, sprawl the most and New York the least. Another group of researchers have suggested eight measurable dimensions such as density, continuity, compactness, and centrality and provided diagrams to explain each one, although it can be hard to tell them apart. Atlanta came out the sprawliest among large metro areas and New York the least sprawly.

Nor does sprawling development occur in the same way in different countries. In the United States developers take large, disconnected chunks of land for housing, shopping malls, and office parks and lobby for new peripheral freeways to repeat the process. Critics call the process leapfrog suburbanization. In Japan, the Tokaido Corridor between Tokyo and Osaka has historically had many extremely small farms whose owners tended to release building lots one or two at a time. The result by the end of the twentieth century was a landscape of small factories and shops, scattered housing, and remnant farmland where city and country "melted" into each other. We might call it retail sprawl in comparison with America's wholesale variety.

Sprawl has been part of the American vocabulary since William H. Whyte's essay on "Urban Sprawl" in *The Exploding Metropolis* in 1959. A landmark report on *The Costs of Sprawl* in 1974 legitimized the term among urban planners and environmentalists. Most often it is a way to vent frustration and mobilize advocates for compact growth, as with Andrés Duany, Elizabeth Plater-Zyberk, and Jeff Speck in *Suburban Nation: The Rise of Sprawl and the Decline of the American Dream* (2000). The term is best used sparingly; like saffron, a small pinch will indelibly color an argument. Suburb and suburbanization are more like salt and pepper, applicable in many times and places.

Chapter 1
The first suburban century

Suburban England did not start out in good repute. Preindustrial suburbs were social fringes of dubious character, dens of ruffians, and haphazard zones of unregulated, noxious, and illicit business. Geoffrey Chaucer gave the Yeoman in the *Canterbury Tales* a short speech about his home in "the suburbes of a toun," which he describes as containing dark corners and blind alleys haunted by robbers and thieves. William Shakespeare's Globe Theatre was in the disreputable suburb of Southwark. In *Henry VIII* he has the Lord Chamberlain, who is trying to keep order on Elizabeth's christening day, complain, "There's a trim rabble let in: are all these your faithful friends o' th' suburbs?" John Milton wrote of "dissolute swordsmen and suburban roysters." In another sixty years the worldly Daniel Defoe, in letter 5 of *A Tour thro' the Whole Island of Great Britain* (1724–27), was not so much appalled by disorder as impressed by London's helter-skelter expansion: "New squares, and new streets rising up every day to such a prodigy of buildings, that nothing in the world does, or ever did, equal it, except old Rome in Trajan's time... [although] it is thus stretched out in buildings, just at the pleasure of every builder, or undertaker of buildings, and as the convenience of the people directs, whether for trade, or otherwise; and this has spread the face of it in a most straggling, confus'd manner, out of all shape, uncompact, and unequal; neither long or broad, round or square."

The situation was indeed changing. In the later eighteenth century, a few men of means built villas along the roads leading out of London and reached their city offices by private coach and then horse-drawn omnibus. In the 1820s a London building boom extended the city westward with the squares and attached houses that are part of uber-stylish Pimlico and Belgravia. John Nash and Decimus Burton were meanwhile designing and building villas within the new Regents Park and elegant attached suburban houses around it. A couple of miles from Charing Cross, St. John's Wood, planned in the 1790s, was now filling with detached and semidetached dwellings. Meanwhile, Edinburgh's New Town was filling in as an upscale neighborhood that was effectively a suburb, physically separated from the cramped and soot-choked medieval city.

Elegant terraces and villas were a transitional stage between the era of suburban roisterers and the modern era of industrial-scale suburbanization. When J. C. Loudon published *The Suburban Gardener, and Villa Companion* (1838) in England and Andrew Jackson Downing published *Cottage Residences* (1842) in the United States, their intended readers were the small set of successful businessmen who could spend working days in the city and make their way to bucolic bliss in their off hours. Their books are the scattered fossils that precede the evolutionary proliferation of the new species named Anglo-American suburb that took its energy from steam. Within a generation, London and Chicago had builders who put up hundreds of houses in a year, and outlying districts counted their annual population growth in the thousands.

Trains and tram lines

The suburbs that play such a major role in contemporary cities were a product of the industrial age and its overlapping eras of steam power in the mid-nineteenth century, electrification at that century's end, and the petroleum era of the twentieth century. The

catalyst for suburbanization was rail-based transportation—
intercity railroads, electric tramways, trolleys, and subways.

Frederick Law Olmsted is a link between the villa era and the
suburban age. Best known as a designer of parks for New York,
Detroit, Montreal, and other cities, he theorized about the
importance of lightening the tensions of city life by providing
access to nature. Large, naturalistic parks that were available to
anyone with Sunday leisure and a streetcar fare, such as Brooklyn,
New York's Prospect Park, were one means. By contrasting with
the artificial city, they would presumably generate a sense of
enlarged freedom. The other way to relieve lowness of spirit was to
create soul-soothing suburbs for frazzled businessmen. The
second goal came to fruition in 1869 in Olmsted's design of
Riverside, a community of curving streets, spacious lots, and
gracious houses that he laid out at a stop on the Chicago,
Burlington and Quincy Railroad eleven miles from the heart of
Chicago. It was to be the best of all worlds, uniting urban and
rural by means of modern transportation. It featured 700 acres of
parks, forty miles of carriage drives, paved roads, its own water
system, gas piped to every home, and a spiffy train depot, all to
serve spacious houses discreetly screened by vegetation. According
to early descriptions, its peaceful green ambiance offered "the
most complete and harmonious suburban effect of the times."

Riverside took early advantage of the nineteenth-century rail
revolution that allowed cities to sort themselves out by economic
class. Upper-crust suburbs were strung like beads along new
intercity railroads—not only Riverside but also Chicago's North
Shore suburbs along the Chicago and Northwestern Railroad;
Philadelphia's Main Line suburbs, named for the trunk line of the
Pennsylvania Railroad; and London suburbs such as Wimbledon
and Surbiton along the London and South Western Railroad.
Boston had Brookline, where Olmsted spent his final decades.
These were bourgeois utopias, in historian Robert Fishman's
memorable phrase. Large houses with room for servants were

nestled among trees and flower beds. Wives stayed home to tend the separate sphere of domestic life. They could consult Catharine Beecher and Harriet Beecher Stowe's book *The American Woman's Home, or Principles of Domestic Science* (1869) for pointers. Fathers caught trains into the city using cut-rate or "commuted" tickets but joined into domestic life on weekends. Harriet Beecher Stowe advised readers of the *Saturday Evening Post* that the new ideal was the "handy man" who could handle tools, tend to household repairs, and even cook a meal if his wife were ill. Residents built substantial churches, organized garden societies, and established tennis and golf clubs. For Anglophilic reasons, proper Philadelphians organized cricket clubs.

Households a notch or three down the economic scale from Brookline and Surbiton could still escape the crowded city core to what historians in the United States call *streetcar suburbs*. Closer to the city center than many bourgeois utopias, or on the wrong side of town, these are areas that horse-drawn street railroads opened to development after 1850 at roughly the same time that a growing middle class was creating a market for new housing. Electrified streetcars or trolleys (the American terms) and tramways (Europe) had even greater impact after 1890. For 6,000 years, cities had depended on walking, which limited their effective radius to two miles, roughly the extent of Rome within its third-century walls. Horse-powered street railways doubled the potential radius, and electric streetcars pushed it further, to six or seven miles. By simple geometry, a city in 1900 had ten times the territory available for development as a city in 1800.

The mechanisms for development varied. When a rural estate or farm outside London came on the market, the developer of a housing estate usually obtained a ninety-nine-year lease and subdivided the land into lots. There was a railway stop not too far away, or at least hopes for one. He might work directly with a large builder to put up houses or sell lots to smaller builders who erected houses a few at a time. Financing came from building societies (similar to American savings and loan associations), insurance companies, individuals with a bit of capital to put to work, and the profits from one set of houses reinvested in another. The results ranged from moderately stylish semidetached houses to monotonous streets of attached two-story houses with tiny back gardens. The Cheap Trains Act of 1883 required railroads to offer a portion of their early-morning trains at cut rates. The Great Eastern Railroad was especially vigorous in complying, serving factories and factory workers on the east side of London, where builders in places like Bexley threw up terraced housing (row housing to Americans) that was affordable to skilled manual workers. The basic plan was two rooms down and two rooms up, with flat facades for cheaper houses and bowed front windows for houses that were a step up.

Camberwell, a chunk of South London beginning about 1.5 miles from London Bridge and extending 4.5 miles into the countryside, epitomizes the evolution of the Victorian suburb. Stages of its development tie to changing transportation options. From the 1770s to the 1830s it attracted men of affairs who took regularly scheduled coaches between their new villas and the city. The horse-drawn omnibus from 1835 to 1862 could carry more riders more cheaply, allowing senior clerks and skilled artisans to seek cleaner suburban air. Horse-drawn tram lines in the 1870s made travel even easier, as did cheap railroad fares after 1883. The northern sections within a few miles of the Thames were now available to working families. In 1830 it was possible to think of Camberwell as a village and parish separate from London, but not for long. The area grew rapidly in the 1830s and 1840s and explosively in the second half of the century. Even as population doubled from 1851 to 1871 and more than doubled from 1871 to 1891, Camberwell districts sorted by social class. Closest to the city center, housing packed more and more densely. Middle-class folks lived 3 and 4 miles out. Higher land farther south remained the domain of larger houses for families with larger incomes, who had moved outward as lower-income families had moved in.

Camberwell was not a tidy suburb of right-angle intersections. Developers purchased leases on fields and estates with irregular boundaries and cut streets as they wished. "That the Victorian suburb was no consciously made artifact is evident enough from a walk along its disjointed streets and from the attempt to find reasonable explanations of the directions some of them took," writes Camberwell's historian. A handful of large builders erected several dozen houses in a year, but typical development was a row of eight houses here, five there, and then four more adjacent to those first eight. Land was cheap enough for Camberwell to grow with street after street of terraced housing and satisfy the English preference for individually owned homes—no Parisian apartments or Manhattan tenements here.

In the United States, land passed from farmer to developer with full title. The major cities of the Atlantic coast took their cues from England. Residents of Philadelphia, Baltimore, and Washington moved into brick-built row houses in new neighborhoods two or three miles from the city center, inner city now but suburban when built. The blocks of brownstone houses on the east side of Manhattan were upscale cousins of Baltimore's row houses, with their white stone stoops, and of London's terraces. Bostonians did it their own way. Streetcar suburbs such as Roxbury filled with New England triple-deckers, buildings with three large dwelling units stacked on each other. With a little capital, a household could build or buy a triple-decker, live in one unit, and rent the other two.

West of the Appalachians, where land was cheap and builders had more elbow room, tracts of small, detached single-family homes were the norm. Immigrant families in Milwaukee lived in two-story houses with daylight basements. Mexican American families on the west side of San Antonio had smaller one-floor houses better suited to the Texas climate. Chicago's S. E. Gross was that city's subdivision king in the 1880s. One of his advertisements trumpeted "The Working Man's Reward. Where All Was Darkness, Now Is Light—A Home at $10.00 a Month." At best, such houses were quite substantial, like the ones that Gross advertised in 1883 in both English and German as "the handsomest brick cottages in Chicago," with ten-foot ceilings on the first floor and eight-foot on the second. At worst, an unscrupulous builder could foist a flimsy house on unsophisticated buyers like the Rudkus family, the Lithuanian immigrants at the center of Upton Sinclair's *The Jungle*, trapping them in debt as it literally fell to pieces around them.

Australia, another country with plenty of elbow room, built its own miles of single-family houses at multiple price points. Federation Era bungalows in aspiring neighborhoods like Mt. Lawley in Perth could be quite substantial (the name derives from the federation of six Australian colonies into a single Commonwealth of Australia in 1901). There were also tracts like the Sydney street described by D. H. Lawrence in *Kangaroo* (1923), a novel based on a three-month excursion from one side of the country to another.

> Murdoch Street [not the actual Sydney street] was an old sort of suburb, little squat bungalows with corrugated tin roofs, painted red. Each little bungalow was set in its own hand-breadth of ground surrounded by a little wooden palisade fence. And there went the long street, like a child's drawing, the little square bungalows dot-dot-dot, close together and yet apart, like modern democracy, each one fenced round with a square rail fence. The street was wide and strips of grass took the place of kerb-stones. The stretch of macadam in the middle seemed as forsaken as a desert.

"Murdoch Street" was paved, but Australian cities in the early twentieth century also had "Cinderella suburbs" of small cottages strung haphazard along dusty "heartbreak streets" waiting for local authorities to notice and bring pavement and sewer lines.

1. Samuel Eberly Gross was one of Chicago's most important homebuilders in the late nineteenth century, responsible for 10,000 houses in twenty-one subdivisions in both working-class and middle-class districts. He vigorously advertised his tracts of standardized houses to households that hoped for the stability and respectability of homeownership.

Lawrence does not mention a tram line, but electric street railroads were ubiquitous in the early twentieth century. In North America they were tools of land speculation as much as travel options. In Los Angeles, the Southern Pacific trolley system notoriously ran lines far out into open country to benefit speculative developers, who would run excursion trains to promote their new subdivisions. Similarly, many of the streetcar lines in Edmonton, Calgary, and Winnipeg were probes into the outback that waited for customers to appear. While waiting, companies often built amusement parks at the end of their lines to generate Sunday fares. London railroads helped builders by advertising the new housing estates that went up near their outlying stations.

Electrified transportation transformed Buenos Aires during its boom decades from the 1890s to the 1930s. Throngs of immigrants from Mediterranean Europe pushed the population of this Chicago of South America from 300,000 to 3 million. The elite continued to live in apartments and big houses in the city center, but upwardly mobile blue-collar and clerical workers moved to western and southern suburbs. Small two- and three-room houses lined grids of dirt streets extending half a dozen blocks on each side of new tram lines. Neighborhoods developed rich social life around schools and soccer teams (it was Argentina).

Streetcars allowed even modest cities to sort into neighborhoods by status. Investors built four streetcar lines north from the cramped center of Norfolk, Virginia, in the 1890s and land companies platted speculative subdivisions. Colonial Place was typical, three miles out from town on a peninsula that jutted into a tidal inlet. An advertisement in 1907 promised "city and country advantages combined." However, ambitions to be *the* Norfolk neighborhood fell short when other subdivisions opened a little farther out. The company initially required building on double lots, resulting in houses like the "big shingled ten room house...with a view of the estuary" that makes a brief appearance

2. In the 1910s, this trolley line five miles from the center of Portland, Oregon, was attracting speculative commercial buildings. The adjacent blocks would fill with single-family houses and small apartments over the next two decades as the streetcar suburb evolved into an automobile suburb and then an established city neighborhood.

in Leon Uris's legal thriller *QB VII* (1970). When sales lagged, the two-lot requirement went away, opening the way for modest two-story houses for junior naval officers, small businessmen, and skilled workers, as well as four-flat and six-flat apartments. Many of the houses would be divided into apartments during the World War II housing shortage and restored by young professionals and university instructors in the 1960s and 1970s.

The journalist James Agee's ode to a streetcar suburb in another southern city is a literary contrast to *The Jungle*, depicting a neighborhood not too unlike Colonial Place. "Knoxville: Summer of 1915," first published in 1938 and later set for soprano and orchestra by Samuel Barber, recalls the city of Agee's childhood. Agee wrote,

18

We are talking now of summer evenings in Knoxville, Tennessee, in the time I lived there so successfully disguised to myself as a child. It was a little bit sort of block, fairly solidly lower middle class, with one or two juts apiece on either side of that. The houses corresponded: middle-sized gracefully fretted wood houses built in the late nineties and early nineteen hundreds, with small front and side and more spacious back yards, and trees in the yards, and porches. ... The men mostly small businessmen, one or two very modestly executives, one or two worked with their hands, most of them clerical, and most of them between thirty and forty-five. ...

People go by; things go by. A horse, drawing a buggy, breaking his hollow iron music on the asphalt. A streetcar raising its iron moan; stopping, belling and starting; stertorous; rousing and raising again its iron increasing moan and swimming its gold windows and straw seats on past and past and past.

Model T suburbs

The first decades of the twentieth century added automobiles to middle-class transportation options, accelerating growth of new suburbs like the Floral Heights setting described in Sinclair Lewis's *Babbitt*, whose protagonist doted on his new motorcar. Real estate ads in the 1910s were careful to show elegant and perhaps hypothetical houses and often made it clear in their idealized images that new developments were intended for streetcar riders and automobile users alike. In 1920, automobiles were still something extra on the urban scene. National registration of eight million vehicles worked out to one car for every thirteen Americans; your family may not have had a car, but one of your neighbors did. By 1930, the automobile had become a household appliance, with one car for every five people nationwide, one for every four Detroiters, and one for every three residents of Los Angeles.

When they could, Americans in the 1920s celebrated growing mobility by purchasing rather than renting a new house. The impulse to home ownership of many ethnic neighborhoods was repeated and multiplied among the growing American middle class. The federal Departments of Labor and Commerce cooperated in an "Own Your Home" campaign in 1920–2. US Secretary of Commerce Herbert Hoover encouraged the real estate business to standardize building codes and develop uniform grading for construction materials. The YMCA offered courses for would-be homeowners. Better Homes in America, Inc., sponsored conferences, publications, and thousands of local committees that organized "Better Homes Week" activities each April. The results were impressive: the increase from 41 to 46 percent home ownership for nonfarm dwellings meant 3.5 million new home-owning households for the decade. Many were financed with the innovation of long-term self-amortizing loans, which offered a measure of protection for homebuyers.

Suburban housing increasingly was mass produced. Electric utilities promoted electric lighting, toasters, and vacuum cleaners (George F. Babbitt's god was "modern appliances.") The single North American market created by a railroad system that reached its maximum around 1920 made it feasible to ship standardized plumbing fixtures, precut molding, and finished doors and windows across the continent. Carpenters became framers and assemblers who put together houses from precut lumber rather than craftsmen who built from scratch. The kit houses that Sears, Roebuck distributed from mills in places like Saginaw, Michigan, were the extreme, arriving with every piece of wood numbered and ready to put together like a giant jigsaw puzzle.

Suburban Britain boomed as well. The Addison Act (1919) implemented Prime Minister David Lloyd George's election slogan "Homes Fit for Heroes" by mandating that local governments take greater responsibility for housing and providing funds, the first of several programs to prime production. Between the wars local governments built more than a million council houses. Their cottage estates filled with terraced

3. Large-scale public and private construction in the 1920s and 1930s substantially upgraded the quality of British housing. These "ten-shilling houses" or "sunshine houses" in the planned community of Bournville outside Birmingham date from 1930. The name comes from their affordable rent and their orientation to maximize natural light.

and semidetached houses with stripped-down Georgian façades. Private builders erected another 2.5 million houses, providing some with extra rooms and bay windows to provide a touch of class. Their market was the increasing number of workers with salaried positions and regular hours that made commuting feasible. London's semidetached suburbia still rode the rails *and* took the bus. Greenfield suburbs developed around new stations as the Tube lines from central London came up for air and extended into the countryside. The process was not much different from the extension of Los Angeles following the lines of the "red electric" streetcars.

Builders and buyers in English-speaking countries shared an international suburban language that they spoke with local accents. "Bungalow," for example, is both a specific housing type with origins in India and a catchall for millions of modest one- or one-and-a-half-story houses built from the 1910s to the 1930s. Chicago's bungalow belt is a crescent of outer-city wards filled with street after street of modest brick houses with sunny front rooms that Chicagoans have identified with the white working class since the 1920s. Denver's brick bungalows have open porches rather than enclosed vestibules and daylight basements as refuges from the extremes of the Great Plains climate. Seattleites built bungalows of wood. Vancouverites might add "English" touches like half-timbering. Australians used the term for one-story houses with sweeping roofs and wide verandas and the tinned-roofed cottages of D. H. Lawrence. As in Britain, the term can be applied colloquially to any unprepossessing one-story house, such as a generic ranch in the United States.

North Americans who wanted a more elegant home built a middle-class suburbia of Dutch colonial, Georgian revival, and "stockbroker Tudor" houses, exactly the sort of neighborhood where John Updike's character Rabbit Angstrom in *Rabbit Is Rich* chooses to live after he inherits a car dealership. Penn Park, as Updike snidely describes it, is home to the city's most ambitious doctors and pushiest insurance agents. Penn Park represented a familiar community type, like Druid Hills in Atlanta or Chestnut Hill in Philadelphia. A well-traveled visitor to Auckland's "leafy suburbs" of Mt. Eden and Remuera might have remarked on the similarities to Edgbaston in Birmingham and Shaughnessy in Vancouver, intended particularly for Canadian Pacific Railroad executives. These lots were larger than those in bungalow belts and the amenities more upmarket, much more like Riverside than like one of S. E. Gross's housing tracts.

Developers in the new automotive era were especially eager to lay out completely new communities for the top 20 percent. The Country Club District in Kansas City attracted international attention. Jesse C. Nichols began to market lots in 1922 for what grew into a 6,000-acre community with four golf clubs, thirty-three distinct subdivisions, and 6,000 homes. Nichols provided parks, a quarter million dollars in artworks to enliven the street corners, and Country Club Plaza, the first large shopping center planned around and for the automobile. Residents in each neighborhood elected board members for homeowners' associations that enforced the development's regulations, maintained parks and playgrounds, and promoted community spirit within the context of comprehensive controls on individual use of property. Shaker Heights, on 1,400 acres east of Cleveland, was another example. Developer-tycoons Oris and Mantis Van Sweringen planned the new town with rigorous internal controls to separate houses by price level. They also separated the major automobile arteries from the tastefully curving residential streets, set aside parklands, prohibited duplexes, and imposed strict architectural controls. The price of choice lots reached $20,000 in 1929 (the equivalent of $300,000 in 2021). Palos Verdes Estates on a hillside overlooking the Pacific was a Southern California equivalent.

Places like Shaker Heights exacerbated a particular American problem. Many of the new upscale suburbs lay outside the boundaries of the core city, often in politically independent suburban municipalities. Alamo Heights literally looked down at San Antonio, Oakwood at Dayton, and Beverly Hills at Los Angeles. These suburban enclaves drew the business elite out of the city. They still owned real estate and operated factories in the city and expected to exert control from banks and corporate boardrooms, but they did not have to experience the consequences of their choices in their domestic lives. They wanted to maintain low city taxes and a stable work environment for their businesses. However, they were increasingly indifferent to the quality of central-city schools, parks, and social services. Ninety percent of Detroit's leading families lived within the city limits in 1910. By the early 1930s, the growth of Grosse Pointe and other suburban towns cut the city's share of the elite to 50 percent. In the early twenty-first century, aerial photographs showed a social and political fault line at the Detroit/Grosse Pointe city line, with abandonment and disinvestment on one side and comfortable life as usual on the other.

The Great Depression, rather surprisingly, stimulated suburban growth in England. Land and construction costs dropped while the salaries of civil servants, middle managers, technicians, and skilled workers held relatively steady, and investors shifted their money toward real estate as a safe haven. There were freestanding villas for the upper middle class, often advertised as nestling among fields and forest even when they were a stone's throw from the rail station and a set of Elizabethan-styled shops, but the 1920s and 1930s were the heyday of the semidetached house. A relatively large semidetached provided privacy, nice interior finishes, a garden large enough to putter in, and the appeal of "a well-ordered and comfortable life"—albeit with very little for wives to do outside the home, leading social workers to worry about "suburban neurosis."

The outlook was not so good for American suburbs. Housing prices plummeted. The number of single-family housing starts in the United States plunged by 75 percent from 1929 to 1933. Overly ambitious subdivisions around Chicago and Detroit lay vacant in a pattern that would repeat on the edge of Sun Belt cities after the crash of 2008. Novelist James Cain incorporated 1929 into the backstory for *Mildred Pierce* (1941). In the 1920s Herbert Pierce had become "a community builder, a man of vision, a big shot," by turning his 300-acre ranch on the edge of Glendale, California, into Pierce Homes. The new Spanish bungalows with white walls and red-tile roofs, with red velvet drapes inside and avocado trees in the front yards, helped to transform Glendale from a "scrubby village" to "an endless suburb, bearing the same relation to Los Angeles as Queens bears to New York." Pierce Homes brought him wealth in the 1920s, but sagging demand drove Pierce and his project into bankruptcy by 1931, leaving his wife to fend for herself over the course of the novel.

It is possible to read the history of early American suburbs by visiting and comparing what are now their older neighborhoods. One neighborhood has a mix of large houses from the 1890s and smaller houses from the 1920s; another from the 1910s gained cheap 1960s apartments that looked like motels as it slipped in status; still another has scarcely changed in outside appearance from 1930. The preferred housing styles changed with the decades, and one of my nerdy pastimes in Portland is to date blocks as I walk different neighborhoods—an 1890s block, a 1920s block, a 1930s block, an early 1940s block—and then grade myself against city property records. I have been learning to do the same thing in the United Kingdom on periodic visits to the Selly Oak–Bournville district on the south side of Birmingham.

Suburban improvement

In 1899, Londoner Ebenezer Howard published a blockbuster book entitled *Tomorrow, a Peaceful Path to Real Reform*. Howard was a court stenographer by day and a sort of tinkerer with ideas by night, crafting ideas about cities rather than building birdhouses. Several years in the United States had widened his horizons and introduced him to Henry George's argument that society rather than individual speculators should benefit from the increased value of land that came with growing population and economic activity. In London he frequented nonconformist reform circles and attended meetings and lectures about democratic socialism. Edward Bellamy's optimism about combining technological progress and social reform in his bestselling utopian novel *Looking Backward* (1890) made a deep impression.

Tomorrow addressed London's intense overcrowding with a proposal for innovative town planning. Independent satellite cities should ring London beyond a protected greenbelt of rural land. Radial rail lines would connect them to the city, and a ring railroad would tie each to the others. Each Garden City should be largely self-contained, with community facilities at its center, industry at its edge, and farmland beyond that. Much of the book's impact came from its diagrams that gave visual shape to the proposal in best utopian fashion. There was the entire metropolitan constellation of city and six symmetrically placed satellites; a close-up showed one possible city plan. Howard insisted that the diagrams were conceptual illustrations, but readers found it easy to take them as specific plans. Another diagram showed the three magnets of town, country, and town–country, with "the people" being slowly drawn toward the third, where they would find freedom and cooperation in a community with "bright homes and gardens, no smoke, no slums." City and country would be harmoniously in balance, Howard wrote. "We should have a cluster of cities . . . so grouped around a Central City that each inhabitant of the whole group, though in one sense living in a town of small size, would in reality be living in and would enjoy the advantages of a great and most beautiful city, and yet all the delights of the country would be within a few minutes' walk."

Howard was a social reformer foremost, not a town planner. In his most memorable phrasing, "town and country must be married, and out of this joyous union will spring a new hope, a new life, a new civilization." His intent was for ownership of the land for a Garden City to initially rest with a public interest corporation headed by very respectable gentlemen. There would be no speculative profits. As the town grew and land values increased, the proceeds from land sales were to be used for community facilities and improvements, keeping taxes low and benefiting everyone. Unfortunately, the importance of "cooperation" was easy to overlook because it was harder to diagram. There is something painful in Howard's practical decision to change the emphasis in the book title from "peaceful path to real reform" in the first edition to the more prosaic *Garden Cities of Tomorrow* (1902) in the second.

Nobody built a Garden City in the first half of the twentieth century because full realization required too much land and too much capital, provided either by a government or a very wealthy benefactor. However, enthusiasts did create garden suburbs as reform-minded architects signed onto the cause. The prototype was Letchworth, begun with Howard's involvement in 1905 on 4,000 acres donated by wealthy industrialists. The Garden City Pioneer Company acquired the land and First Garden City Ltd. engaged architects Raymond Unwin and Barry Parker to lay out the site thirty-three miles from London. They planned a town square, housing in arts and crafts style that recalled rural cottages, industrial sites on the edge, and an encompassing greenbelt. It was an undoubted success as a sort of beta test for an idea with broad appeal, even if it was easy to ridicule for the earnest vegetarians and teetotalers it attracted. A few years later Unwin promoted Howard's ideas in *Nothing Gained by Overcrowding! How the Garden City Type of Development May Benefit Both Owner and Occupier*, illustrated with more diagrams and photographs contrasting cramped housing built according to official bylaws with lovely garden suburbs.

Germany was fertile ground for Garden City ideas. It was a leader in city planning and engineering, and Garden Cities appealed simultaneously to experts desiring rational city planning, to industrialists who wanted contented workers, to architects who wanted to practice modern efficiency, and, from a quite different standpoint, to nationalists who saw them as a means to affirm traditional values. Dozens of garden suburbs sprouted from German soil. The best known was Römerstadt, an affordable "daughter town" outside the mother city of Frankfurt that combined modernist architecture and Garden City planning.

British architects associated with the movement embarked on ocean voyages to take garden suburbs or facsimiles around the world. Howard actively promoted his ideas and helped to create an International Garden Cities and Town Planning Association in 1913. Letchworth had attracted residents with socialist leanings, but many other international imitations aimed at the aspiring middle classes. The Garden City district of Cairo featured curving streets and houses designed in French and Italian styles that were popular with the Egyptian and Levantine elite. In São Paulo, architect Barry Parker advised a British land company about developing its holdings in picturesque valleys near the edge of the city. Pacaembu and Jardin América promised the opportunity to enjoy housing like the Anglo-Saxon homes across the Atlantic. Colonel Light Gardens in Adelaide was less posh. The South Australian government purchased 300 acres on the south side of the city to build a model garden suburb with the standard features of curving streets, spaces for shops and churches, and lots for single-family bungalows. Twenty years after it was finished, the neighborhood featured in *Australia and Your Future: Your Christmas under the Sun*, a 1947 film aimed to lure migrants from Britain.

Americans blended Garden City ideas into an ongoing argument for metropolitan decentralization. Several of the nation's leading planners and intellectuals in the 1920s called themselves the Regional Planning Association of America and worked to promote the development of a "middle landscape" that combined the creative energies of the city and the residential environment of the country or small town. The New York State Commission of Housing and Regional Planning advocated for the dispersed and balanced development of an entire state, with power delivered by an electric grid and transportation over modern roads. Lewis Mumford, the Regional Planning Association of America's best-known spokesman, called for "a more satisfactory layout, region by region, with countryside and city developed together for the purpose of promoting and enhancing the good life." The glue between city and country could be garden towns and suburbs.

These evangelistic architects and planners tried their hand in Radburn, New Jersey. Just across the new George Washington Bridge from Manhattan, it had forty- to sixty-acre superblocks, with front doors turned toward interior parks and pedestrians separated from automobile traffic. Unfortunately, work began on Radburn in 1928 and full financing was blocked by the Depression. Even so, 1,200 residents (rather than the expected 25,000) found a superior community. Internationally known planner John Nolen had similar goals for Mariemont near Cincinnati, which he called "a new town built to produce local happiness." Although the town was funded by a philanthropist to give industrial workers homes away from the looming shadows of the factory district, the result was closer to a well-designed, middle-class suburb.

The culmination of the garden suburb enthusiasm in the United States were three "greenbelt towns" that the federal government built on the outskirts of Washington (Greenbelt, Maryland), Milwaukee (Greendale, Wisconsin), and Cincinnati (Greenhills, Ohio). The national state was not properly in the business of building civilian communities. However, FDR "brain truster" Rexford Tugwell found a workaround by using the Resettlement Administration, an agency that was intended to help displaced farm families. Initial plans for nine towns shrank with local opposition and tight budgets, but the three survivors were ready at the end of the 1930s. Greenbelt, the best known, had a central lake and park, a tasteful community shopping center, and a mix of duplexes, townhouses, and apartments. Residents were carefully screened Washingtonians, many of them lower-level government employees; fear of upsetting Southern Congresspeople meant that Black families need not apply. Along with Radburn, it featured as an exemplary suburb in the film *The City*, funded by the Institute of American Planners and shown at the New York World's Fair of 1939.

After 1945, greenbelt towns shared a common fate with two other federally built communities built to serve the nuclear weapons program. Los Alamos, New Mexico, and Richland, Washington, were isolated, freestanding communities built for the scientists, engineers, and skilled workers who designed the first atomic bombs and produced fissionable plutonium. Whether on a high mesa or the bank of the Columbia River, however, their planners drew on the same ideas implemented at Palos Verdes and Greenbelt, making them middle-class suburbs without a city. By the early 1950s, an increasingly conservative Congress decided to get the federal government out of the domestic suburb business and privatized the communities despite substantial local opposition. Even then, the US government was exporting its suburban model in the form of aid programs and military bases.

Chapter 2
Suburbs at flood tide

I grew up in a 1950s suburb. We lived in a new Dayton, Ohio, neighborhood where every house was of the same vintage. I walked to a shiny new elementary school that was not even finished when I started and that kept expanding as more baby boom kids arrived to move through its eight grades. A new strip mall had a grocery, a dry cleaner, and a drug store that sold me Scrooge McDuck comic books and plastic model kits. Summer evenings we tuned the radio to listen to Cincinnati Reds games while fireflies blinked in the small backyard. Dads drove off to work and moms stayed home to keep busy with bridge games, church, or the League of Women Voters.

Dayton's College Hill neighborhood was part of a suburban wave that spread outward from every city in the United States, Canada, Australia, and the British Isles in the decades after World War II. Tens of millions of new houses, schools, and shopping centers gave white-collar and blue-collar families an alternative to small towns and city apartments. The same neighborhoods were also homogeneous, preserving racial and sometimes ethnic and religious hierarchies. One essential story of the postwar suburbs was certainly the construction of new communities that served the needs of millions of families. A second story, however, has been the ways in which that sense of community has often depended on racial exclusion. A third story has been the more recent transformation of many suburbs into vibrantly multiethnic places.

Station wagon suburbs

Canada's postwar neighborhoods are peppered with Victory Houses built between 1943 and 1960. What was initially a prefab design by Wartime Housing Limited for housing for war workers in Toronto, Ottawa, and Halifax became a template for both private builders and Central Mortgage and Housing, the national housing agency. Victory Houses boosted homeownership and single-family suburbia from North York (Toronto) to Richmond (Vancouver). The small, square houses provided 1,000 square feet of space in four rooms down and two rooms up under a pitched roof. Sometimes called "strawberry box houses" in a style that would soon be challenged by one-story ranch houses, they accommodated hundreds of thousands of young families who could easily expand and personalize the house as time and money allowed.

Houses in Levittown, New York, looked a lot like Victory Houses. Arthur Levitt and Sons specialized in the efficient production of affordable housing. The company's first Levittown, in Nassau County, Long Island, east of New York City, was empty land at the start of 1947. It counted 51,000 residents in 15,000 identical houses by the end of 1950. For $8,000 (later $9,000), a young family got a basic 750-square-foot home with four rooms and an attic space that weekend handymen could turn into additional living space. A second Levittown, outside Philadelphia, sold 3,500 houses in ten weeks. It was a bit spiffier, with prices ranging from $9,000 for the smaller "rancher" model to $17,500 for the expensive "country club" style. At $10,900, the "jubilee" came with two full baths, push-button ranges, all-steel kitchen cabinets, and twenty-three pieces of shrubbery. Other Levittowns followed in New Jersey and, in 1963, outside San Juan, Puerto Rico, where the good life began (*donde la buena vida comienza*) in the three-bedroom Diadema model or the four-bedroom Esmeralda.

Victory House neighborhoods and Levittowns were early steps in the creation of the "station wagon suburbs" where tens of millions of the baby boom generation grew up and returned to raise their families. In aggregate by the crudest census measure, the United States became a majority suburban nation by 2000. These postwar suburbs were variations on a familiar theme, with freeways rather than trolleys making more and more peripheral land available for new housing and new communities. Newer suburbs sorted by economic class, as older suburbs had in previous generations. On the unfashionable "wrong" side of the metropolis were smaller, poorly serviced subdivisions without the tax base to pay for good schools. On the "good" side of the metropolis were politically independent towns with large lot subdivisions, no apartments, and more expensive houses. Between the extremes were generic "sitcom suburbs" like the one where I grew up.

4. The suburbanization of the United States in the second half of the twentieth century required massive investment not only in highways and housing but also in schools, parks, and playgrounds. These children in Westchester County, north of New York City, are members of the millennial generation, who followed the baby boom generation and Generation X.

The federal government played important roles in American suburbanization. The Federal Housing Administration began insuring low down payment loans in 1934, expanding homeownership while using criteria that disadvantaged Black buyers (the National Housing Act in Canada played a similar role in expanding ownership through standardized and insured loans). The Veterans Administration added its own mortgage program, which guaranteed loans by private lenders and allowed veterans to buy with no down payment. The programs drew private capital into housing production to satisfy demand that had gone unmet during the war, as well as the needs of millions of Americans who formed new families. The new suburbs accommodated the American taste for detached, single-family homes. The nation built fourteen million of them from 1946 through 1960, compared to approximately two million new apartment units. The proportion of households that owned or were buying their own homes rose from 44 percent in 1944 to 62 percent in 1960; it continued to grow at a slower pace into the next century, reaching 69 percent before the housing market crashed in 2007. In Canada, the National Housing Act similarly facilitated homeownership by insuring standardized mortgages.

The federal government not only made it easy for developers to erect and sell suburban houses, but also made it possible for people to live in them. Few residents noticed the underground infrastructure of water mains and sewage treatment systems that federal grants helped to fund, but everyone saw the above-ground freeways. The Federal Aid Highway Act of 1956 committed the nation to the largest building program in its history. Construction of 41,000 miles of interstate and defense highways was the rough equivalent of digging sixty Panama Canals. The system would connect nine of ten American cities of 50,000 or more residents with multilane, limited-access freeways. Half of the estimated cost was for the 5,500 miles that would cut directly across urban areas.

Urban freeways were planned in the 1950s but built in the 1960s, 1970s, and 1980s. They were intended to shore up downtowns and to increase the value and accessibility of suburban land, which proved to be the greater success. The standard design is a cross and circle. Long-distance interstates converge on the city center, and an outer circumferential loop diverts long-distance traffic around the city. With local variations, it fits cities from Atlanta to Indianapolis to Wichita. The loop also connects suburbs to each other, in an ironic replication of Ebenezer Howard's scheme for Garden Cities distributed around a ring railroad. The loop is the iconic anchor of late-twentieth-century suburbs, whether locals call it the Capital Beltway (Washington), the Perimeter (Atlanta), the Orbital (London), Boulevard Périphérique (Paris), or variations on ring road (Berlin, Brussels, Beijing).

Although the intrepid Iain Sinclair did write *London Orbital: A Walk around the M-25* (2002), suburban freeways and ring roads are unromantic objects of greatest interest to the real estate industry. They compound the earlier effects of rail transit by opening vast swathes of countryside to development. In the United States that has meant larger houses on larger lots. The average size of a new single-family house was around 1,000 square feet in the 1950s but 1,660 in 1973, the first year that the Census Bureau compiled such data. Forty-two years later, the average size peaked at 2,687 square feet. At the American extreme were subdivisions with half-acre lots for oversized and overly elaborate houses sometimes derided as McMansions.

Other English-speaking nations have followed a similar path. Canadians have been very enthusiastic homeowners, especially in such Prairie Province cities as Calgary, Edmonton, and Winnipeg, which had higher ownership rates in the 2010s than Los Angeles or Dallas. Automobile ownership and homeownership shot up in tandem in postwar Australia. Sydney homeownership soared from 40 percent to 70 percent from 1947 to 1961, outpointing even the United States. Housing also got bigger with a growth trajectory that closely parallels that of the United States (or is it the other way around?). Late-twentieth-century Australia was a suburban

5. In the early twenty-first century, the population of greater Tokyo was larger than that of metropolitan London and New York combined. As an alternative to freeway suburbanization, public transit with more than 1,000 train and subway stations carries well over half of all trips. The lines were notoriously overcrowded in the boom years of the 1970s and 1980s, but much less so in the 2020s.

culture marked by the icons of barbecues and Holden station wagons. Australian houses followed a nearly identical growth curve, as three-quarters of the residents of its five largest metropolitan areas lived in automobile-dependent suburbs.

Dubliners shared the suburban taste. New residents with deep roots in rural Ireland arrived with a preference for their own house with gardens front and back. Builders responded with suburban estates on open land and the outskirts of small towns. Some were upscale, some a bit down market, as novelist Tana French described "Knocknaree" in *In the Woods* (2007): "Picture an orderly little maze of houses on a hill, only a few miles from Dublin. Someday, the government had declared, this will be a buzzing marvel of suburban vitality, a plan-perfect solution to overcrowding and poverty and every urban ill; for now [mid-1980s] it is a few handfuls of cloned semi-detached, still new enough to look startled and gauche on their hill side." As the Irish economy took off toward the end of the century, most of Dublin's new housing estates were between fifteen and twenty-five miles from the city center, often encircling small towns. Tana French was writing a police procedural and needed an ominous atmosphere, but residents of real Dublin suburbs have told researchers that they especially like the pastoral feel of "a semi-rural location with the city of Dublin on my doorstep," in the words of an informant from the booming commuter town of Ratoath in County Meath, eighteen miles from Dublin's city center.

Private developers in Britain built for the upper economic strata in the postwar decades while local governments built 1.6 million council houses, most now transferred to private ownership. "Bevan houses," named for charismatic cabinet member Aneurin Bevan, were upgrades from prewar standards and served a similar role in Victory Houses and Levittown starters. Because of Britain's adoption of greenbelt and New Town plans, suburban development has been more concentrated than in the United States or Canada, with new housing filling in established suburbs, building out new satellites, and engulfing small towns beyond protected green areas.

In her novel *Arlington Park* (2006), Rachel Cusk encapsulates a century of suburban growth around a provincial city. In the city center, a man with dreadlocks waits for the bus to his run-down Victorian suburb, beyond which the route would lead to warehouses, superstores, and office parks. Up the hill we pass from Victorian suburbia to interwar and postwar neighborhoods for the comfortable classes: "The buildings grew more graceful and the pavements more orderly. As the road ascended to Arlington Park the big, brash shops down below were succeeded by florists and antique shops; the off-licenses became wine merchants, the fast-food chains became bistros. To either side tree-lined streets began to appear." In turn, a housewife from Arlington Park, on her way to the massive Merrywood mall at an equally massive motorway interchange, has the satisfaction of superiority to newer suburbs and the "unrelieved symmetry of their long, straight residential roads, each one showing its vista of identical houses and front gardens and driveways protruding like little paved tongues." Cusk is a sharp social observer, and her unnamed city is a transatlantic cousin to John Updike's Brewer, Pennsylvania, built with a British accent.

New Towns

The prewar Garden City was the hardy intellectual rootstock on which postwar Europe grafted a variety of ideas and plans for New Towns. Governments in several countries liked the idea of building complete satellite towns to absorb growing metropolitan populations. The effort came closer to realizing Ebenezer Howard's scheme for metropolitan regions than had prewar garden suburbs. Britain went with New Towns in a big way, creating twenty in two waves. Sweden was simultaneously part of the first wave, and France and the United States were in the second. Though the New Town impulse damped down in the Atlantic world by the 1990s, East Asian countries have taken it into a third wave.

European New Towns varied according to national expectations about housing. English families did not like the idea of someone living on top of them, so their New Towns were low-rise expanses of semidetached and detached houses. To no one's surprise, later New

Towns in the United States were equally low slung. People on the Continent were more accustomed to apartment living, so their governments tended to build at higher densities. The same would be true of the East Asian New Towns of the twenty-first century.

British New Towns were a utopian project, built out of the desires for orderly metropolitan growth, preservation of green landscapes, replacement of dreadfully substandard housing, and modernization of industry—all within an expanding welfare state. Their prophet was Patrick Abercrombie and his manifesto was the *Greater London Plan* of 1944. Drawing on decades of regional planning and Garden City ideas, he proposed a five-ring metropolis of city core, denser suburbs, newer suburbs, wide greenbelt, and New Towns beyond in the fields of Sussex, Essex, Berkshire, and Hertfordshire. The Labour government started a total of fourteen New Towns around London and Glasgow between 1946 and 1950. Stevenage, thirty miles north of London, was typical of the first wave, designed to the most up-to-date planning ideals with an automobile-free commercial center and superblocks enclosing neighborhood units that scaled up Radburn, New Jersey, but with terrace housing. A second New Town wave in the 1960s designated several existing towns like Peterborough, east of London, and Redditch, south of Birmingham, as growth poles for housing and commercial investment.

New Towns were controversial. They absorbed farmland and necessarily overlaid or absorbed small towns, to the distress of local residents. The government did a hard sell to convince deep-dyed city dwellers to pioneer in the countryside, making films and featuring New Towns in the Festival of Britain (1951), which celebrated emergence from wartime and postwar austerity. The town center for Cumbernauld, Scotland, was strikingly modern, snaking along a ridgeline, but typical New Towners lived in traditional terraced and semidetached houses. Buildings and infrastructure have not always aged well, but neither have many other suburbs of the same age around Europe and the Americas.

If Britain was a New Town proving ground, Sweden was the urban planner's ideal. The city of Stockholm owned outlying land, built and operated the transit system, and was responsible for regional planning and public housing. Its New Town of Vallingby was a mid-rise utopia that did the prewar garden suburbs of Britain and the United States one better. Vallingby was clean, convenient, close to the countryside, and community centered. It was a sensation among planners, architects, and policy makers who were trying to guide European reconstruction in the early 1950s; the town hired multilingual "Miss Vallingby" tour guides to keep up with the visitors.

European New Towns intrigued Americans, but they were not going to reproduce Sweden's social democratic apartment communities or follow Britain's lead with a dozen government-built towns. They could, however, look to Finland, where Tapiola had undeniable appeal. A decade after Vallingby, a large nonprofit Housing Foundation rather than the central government built the New Town six miles from Helsinki. It was organized into community clusters centered on a town center with a single high-rise office building. Low-rise apartments and row houses for 20,000 residents nestled in the Finnish forest. It was "a small town in unspoiled country, pointing a new way to build modern communities," said its architect. In fact, it bore a family resemblance to Greenbelt, Maryland, but with different trees and more snow.

American planners and critics delighted in Tapiola. Wolf Von Eckardt praised it in the *Washington Post*. Ada Louise Huxtable of the *New York Times* called it the finest of the New Towns. Robert Simon, the businessman who planned and built the first stage of Reston, Virginia, in the mid-1960s, was an admirer. The idea for Reston was familiar—a set of suburban villages and employment centers that would be self-contained but easily accessible to Washington, DC (and to national media, which gave glowing write-ups). The first village center around Lake Anne, completed in 1965–66, had the Tapiola look—winding pedestrian paths, townhouses in the trees, and a community center with a high-rise. Buildout by corporations with deeper pockets has been far less interesting.

Columbia, Maryland, between Washington and Baltimore, was an even larger undertaking that aimed to be a complete New Town with 100,000 residents, all necessary services, and employment centers. Builder James Rouse, who had made a fortune in shopping center development, had a deep-seated and contagious belief that carefully planned New Towns could provide high-quality environments and still turn a profit. By 1980, Columbia housed 53,000 people in an attractive, racially integrated community.

Reston and Columbia were near enough to Capitol Hill to pique the interest of Congress. The New Communities Act (1968) tried to enlist the federal government in the New Towns movement. It guaranteed bonds issued by private developers who agreed to build genuine New Towns, communities that would have people of mixed incomes, social services, and a balance in jobs and housing. Most of the New Towns begun enthusiastically in the years around 1970 crashed to a halt during the 1974 recession, when federal assistance proved far too limited to overcome rising costs and a sagging real estate market. Those New Towns that survived as planned had the advantages of Sun Belt locations and hot real estate markets. The Woodlands, thirty miles north of Houston, housed 10,000 people on 17,000 meticulously planned and controlled acres. Irvine, California, on a single, privately owned tract of 130 square miles between Los Angeles and San Diego, adapted the concept of neighborhood clusters and employment nodes to the automobile culture of the West.

The American government has also built a very distinctive variety of New Towns on foreign soil. The United States has maintained a powerful military presence in Germany, Italy, Japan, South Korea, and other allied nations. Tens of thousands of military personnel and civilian contractors operate and support airfields and supply depots, many with families along. They live in islands of suburbia that one commentator calls "America towns." Inside the gates of the base are residential complexes that would be at home on the outskirts of Columbus or Charlotte. Planned to make Americans feel at home, many are widely spread, auto-oriented expanses of groomed grass and single-family houses with shopping centers, fast-food outlets, and sometimes even golf courses. They are gated company towns in which the US government is the company.

American bases aside, East Asia is the center of New Town action in the twenty-first century. Chinese cities in the new century have used their ownership of peripheral land for New Town (*xincheng*) projects. Some are large-scale planned residential developments and some more fully comprehensive New Towns. Nanjing invested massively in new transit to open the backwater west side of the Yangtze River for Hexi New Town. New infrastructure increases land values that the municipality can capture when it sells parcels to developers. The demolition of old core housing increases the demand for open-market "commodity housing" as displaced families use compensation money to buy older suburban housing, allowing sellers to move out and up into modern flats. In 2021, Shanghai announced a plan to accommodate a million new residents in five New Towns built among farms and factories an hour or so from the city; a stated goal is to avoid becoming Los Angeles.

Seoul's New Towns are tied to national defense policy. The city is only thirty miles from the demilitarized zone. As it grew, the national government worried that unregulated suburbs might grow too close to the zone and adopted the Five New Towns Development Plan in 1989. The Korea Land Development Corporation expropriated tracts of land twelve to fifteen miles from the center of Seoul, and the Korea National Housing Corporation and private developers shared construction of 300,000 apartments for 1.2 million people. Ten smaller New Towns came in the second wave in the twenty-first century.

Bundang is the largest, with 400,000 residents. Closest to the city's very trendy and expensive Gangnam district, it has been highly popular as an upper-middle-class utopia, earning the phrase "Bundang under heaven."

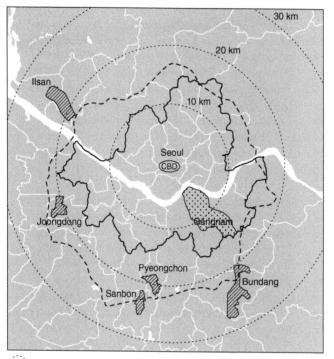

Distance from Seoul CBD

Gyeongboo Expressway

Seoul Outer Circular Expressway, completed in 2007

6. New Towns have been one of the favored planning choices for many European and Asian nations since the mid-twentieth century. In the 1980s, South Korea began to ring Seoul with large New Towns as a way to house the burgeoning metropolis, but with locations chosen with an eye to the proximity of the armistice line not far to the north.

Suburbia and race

My neighborhood on the edge of Dayton, Ohio, was a nice place to grow up, but it also had a complex social dynamic underlying my nostalgic image of flickering fireflies. There was a parochial school only a few blocks away for Roman Catholic kids with whom public school students seldom interacted. There were Jewish families because it was on the liberal side of town, unlike the religiously restricted suburb on the south side. Like many similar neighborhoods, it was also completely white. No Black kids lived nearby, and none went to my elementary school, or even to my (larger) high school. I first shared a classroom with Black students when my high school opened a summer-session geometry class to smart kids from other schools. The small class was superficially friendly, and at age fourteen I did not realize how cautiously and carefully they must have navigated this foreign territory.

Dayton was typical. Racially integrated neighborhoods were rare in cities and even more scarce in suburbs. As elsewhere around the nation, federal highway construction and infrastructure grants helped to build new suburbs for white families, but discriminatory real estate practices worked to exclude poor people, African Americans, and often other people of color. In the early twentieth century, housing developers often limited who could buy into their new neighborhood by including racial restrictions in the deeds of sale. Although the US Supreme Court ruled in 1948 that such racially restricted covenants were unenforceable, real estate salespeople continued to actively steer Black homebuyers away from white suburbs and toward those that already had large Black populations, such as on Atlanta's west side.

Such discrimination becomes deeply entrenched when public land use regulations are controlled at the local level. Exclusionary zoning refers to regulations that limit multifamily housing while requiring large lots and extensive amenities that raise the cost of single-family houses. Such regulations, which look like they are "color-blind," are actually tools of segregation that defend class and racial privilege by making housing too expensive for most lower-income families. White homeowners could convince themselves that they were protecting property values and community character and nothing else, a narrative that suburban politicians were happy to embrace. One consequence has been to deprive many nonwhite Americans of the opportunity to build wealth through investment in stable suburban communities.

It is not that every suburb was white, but that few were integrated. From the early twentieth century Black Americans developed their own suburban communities on the sides of town that the white real estate market ignored, and large Black communities developed in suburbs and satellite cities such as Pasadena, California. Black suburbanization continued in the station wagon era, often the result of the Black side of a city growing outward beyond municipal borders—beyond Atlanta's west side into Fulton County or from northeast Washington into Prince George's County, Maryland, which was 60 percent Black by the 1990s. In an affluent metropolitan area like Washington, many Prince George's neighborhoods were indistinguishable from middle-class white suburbia. Other stretches of Black suburbia were less fortunate, since developers seldom favored them with the glitzier malls and upscale office parks. In a nation where property taxes are essential to local government, the white suburbs got richer but Black suburbs did not, making it that much harder for middle-class families than for their white counterparts to leave behind the problems of poverty-stricken neighborhoods. The wave of inner-city gentrification that impacted many cities after 2000 exacerbated the same problem by pushing more Black and Latino households to suburbs.

White South Africans were neither as self-deluded nor as subtle as Americans, although segregationist ideas circulated from one country to the other. In the early twentieth century, San Francisco officials had considered moving that city's Chinese population to an industrial suburb. Municipal governments in cities like Cape

Town, Durban, and Johannesburg acted as well as contemplated, using the excuse of public health to force nonwhites out of city centers to informal communities such as the so-called slum belt that cupped Johannesburg on the south. Continued urban growth and the desire for greater residential segregation in turn made these semisuburbs targets for wholesale clearance and population relocation. In a notorious example, in 1955 South African authorities used thousands of police to evict residents from Sophiatown, a thriving center of Black life for more than four decades that had nurtured the careers of musicians Hugh Masekela and Miriam Makeba.

The alternatives for nonwhite South Africans were Black townships beyond the urban fringe. Fifty years of efforts to police white–Black interactions culminated in the apartheid regime of 1948–84. Hendrick Verwoerd's Department of Native Affairs administered the absolute racial zoning of the Group Areas Act (1950). The goal was to replace segregation by city neighborhoods with separation of white city and nonwhite suburbs. Johannesburg in the 1950s expanded smaller Black townships into a massive set of new communities fifteen miles southwest of the city. A single road led from each township into the city, crossing a wide expanse of open land that some nicknamed the "machine gun belt." The government provided matchbox houses and sometimes simply a concrete slab; the common NE 51/6 house plan stood for "non-European 1951 design 6." Soweto, for Southwestern Township, is the best known. At the turn of the twenty-first century, a crude description of Johannesburg geography was white suburbs on its north and Black suburbs or townships on its south.

Twenty-first-century diversity

During the 2020 US presidential campaign, Donald Trump proclaimed himself the protector of the suburbs, and a speaker at the Republican National Convention charged that the Democrats "want to abolish the suburbs forever by ending single-family home zoning." As pundits quickly pointed out, the president held an image of all-white middle-class suburbia that no longer existed. American suburbs are now multiracial, although not necessarily integrated at fine grain. They have large numbers of poor people as well as the affluent. There are plenty of "traditional" cul-de-sac neighborhoods, but there are also millions of two-story apartments near freeway interchanges and shopping malls filled with young couples, unattached singles, and struggling families.

They are magnets for immigrants. In both Canada and the United States, twenty-first-century immigrants from Asia, Latin America, and Africa have headed directly to suburbs, where there is a variety of affordable housing and communities of fellow nationals that are the more dispersed version of the inner-city immigrant neighborhoods of the previous century. More than half of the residents of suburban Markham, Brampton, and Mississauga that ring Toronto are "visible minorities," the term used by Statistics Canada. On the other coast, immigrants fill Richmond and Burnaby south and east of Vancouver. A *Vancouver Sun* analysis in 2015 claimed that one Burnaby census tract is North America's most diverse neighborhood. The area's Member of Parliament reports attending ten events in a single day in the riding or electoral district, each featuring a different ethnic group and language—Tagalog, Tamil, Korean, Japanese, Hungarian, Romanian, Punjabi, Serbian, Mandarin, Cantonese, French (the language of many residents from Africa), and more.

Nor are London's suburbs as white as they have often appeared on television screens. The charming film *Bend It Like Beckham* (2004) follows the friendship and challenges of two teenage girls, one from a white English family and one from a Sikh family, as they pursue their dreams of soccer stardom. Jess Bharma, the girl of South Asian heritage, is from Hounslow, an established middle-class London suburb that has steadily grown more diverse, like other districts five to fifteen miles from the city center. Southhall, for example, was majority Asian by 2021. Zadie Smith's novel *White Teeth* (2000) centers on the friendship of three classmates of white, Bangladeshi, and Jamaican heritage in the inner suburb of Willesden, with minor characters to fill out the ethnic variety of the metropolis.

Observers looking for diversity in another great Atlantic city usually head to New York's borough of Queens, but Westchester County offers perhaps unexpected lessons. Located immediately north of New York City, it was long a prime setting for primetime shows featuring white suburbanites. *The Dick Van Dyke Show*'s Rob Petrie lived in New Rochelle. The title character in *Maude* lived in Tuckahoe. Dan Draper in *Mad Men* lived in Ossining. In the last season of *Friends*, Monica and Chandler marked a life transition by moving north from Manhattan to Westchester. The county may have been prototypical white suburbia in 1960, but now fewer than half of the county's dwelling units are single-family houses. A quarter of its population is foreign born; non-Hispanic whites like Monica and Chandler are only a slight majority.

The first thing that the former president missed was the rise of suburban poverty. Where central city boundaries are fixed, many sixty- and seventy-year-old neighborhoods are suburban by definition. These are often hand-me-down neighborhoods; previous residents age out or move out and the houses "filter down" to new and likely lower-income households. The process accelerates when the trendy middle class rediscovers inner-city neighborhoods and pushes the low-income families outward.

Suburban homogeneity also eroded because suburbs have experienced the demographic changes that have transformed the United States as a whole. In 2020, 45 percent of American suburbanites were people of color, up from 20 percent in 1990. In Los Angeles, the percentage of Black, Indigenous, and people of color residents in the suburbs rather than the city increased from 26 percent in 1970 to 70 percent in 2010. Using the crude division of metropolitan areas into central cities and suburban rings, a majority of every major racial and ethnic group now live in the latter. They are able to enjoy the "wages of suburbia" in the form of better schools, better community facilities, and greater safety.

In the half century after the 1965 Immigration Reform Act opened America's borders, newcomers transformed its suburbs. Television's Nelson family of Ozzie, Harriet, David, and Ricky may be the iconic representative of postwar American suburbanites, but at the mall one is just as likely to run into the Nguyen and Nunez families and their kids. Aggregate statistics conceal suburban mosaics that are as complex as early-twentieth-century New York. The cities of Elgin and Aurora on the west side of Chicago have been home to growing numbers of Puerto Ricans and Mexican Americans since the 1940s, and the majority of Latinos in twenty-first-century Chicagoland are suburbanites. Boston suburbs such as Chelsea, Somerville, and Malden have attracted immigrants from Brazil, Colombia, Haiti, and China. Arlington, Virginia, has become a center for Vietnamese, Cambodians, Ethiopians, Hondurans, Bolivians, and Mexicans. Daly City, the San Francisco suburb that inspired the song "Little Boxes," is now a majority-Asian community with tens of thousands of residents of Filipino heritage. Milpitas, in Santa Clara County, was a white working-class suburb in the 1960s whose industrial jobs were inaccessible to Oakland's minority residents; in the twenty-first century it is another majority–Asian American high-tech suburb. By one measure, zip code 75038 in Irving, Texas, near the Dallas–Fort Worth airport, is the most diverse in the United States, almost evenly divided among Asian, Black, Hispanic, and white residents.

Lakewood, California, remains a touchstone for American suburbia. The all-white suburb of the 1950s is now a multiethnic community of white families, Asian American families, Black families, and Mexican American families. The transition has not always been easy as different groups assert their claims to parks and fill the schools, a change that the essayist D. J. Waldie has watched: "Where I live is one of the places where suburban stories were first mass-produced. They were stories then for displaced Okies and Arkies, Jews who know the pain of exclusion, Catholics who thought they did, and anyone white with a steady job. Today, the same stories begin here, except the anxious people who tell them are completely mixed in their colors and ethnicities. I continue to live here because I want to find out what happens next in the stories I think I already know."

Chapter 3
Vertical suburbs

In 1954, Nikita Khrushchev addressed the national conference of builders, architects, and construction workers of the Soviet Union. A year into his tenure as general secretary of the Communist Party, his challenge was to build a modern industrialized nation, and he wanted an efficient way to house millions of families in burgeoning Soviet cities. Engineers had been testing different construction techniques, including concrete poured on site, but the general secretary left no doubt about the right answer: "We must proceed along the more progressive path—the path of using prefabricated reinforced concrete structures and parts." The statement was met with enthusiastic applause. Millions of identical apartments in three- to five-story walk-up apartment buildings were the result. The standard soon grew to beyond a dozen floors as engineers became more confident and elevators more affordable. On the outskirts of Soviet cities from Vilnius to Vladivostok, millions of families lived in the new standardized buildings that they nicknamed *Khrushchevka* and *Brezhnevka*, in sarcastic homage to Khrushchev and his successor, Leonid Brezhnev.

Suburb is not synonymous with detached and semidetached single-family houses, nor has it always been shaped by Garden City visions. Visit many large cities around the globe and you will see clusters of suburban apartment towers silhouetted against the horizon line like mesas rising in the dry landscape of the American Southwest. This is the case in the *banlieues* of Paris as well as the outskirts of Moscow. It is true of Beijing, Singapore, and Seoul. This distinctive ecology of suburban housing towers—we might call it the Eurasian contrast to Anglo-American suburbs—has usually been the result of deliberate public policies designed to house fast-growing urban populations efficiently and economically. Housing authorities in the United States also built large blocks of public housing, but as inner-city redevelopment projects and at much smaller scale. The suburban high-rise action was European in the later twentieth century, East Asian in the twenty-first.

Eastern Europe's slab suburbs

State-led economic policies in the Soviet Union and its Eastern European allies required state-led housing policies. Large-scale industrialization drew workers and families into the major cities that were already short of housing. The solution was government apartment blocks on the urban fringe, rising in clusters of six- or ten-story buildings with open space and basic services. Standardized apartments in concrete slab buildings were quick and easy to build from the mid-1950s through the 1970s. The ubiquity of their construction technique earned them a common name; where the United States had ranches and split-levels, Czechs have *panelák* and Hungarians have *panelház*.

Eastern Europe's new suburbs wove together several traditions. Soviet architects and planners were enthusiasts for 1920s and 1930s modernism, with its emphasis on creating simple, standardized machines for living and for housing urban residents in towers within parkland. High-rise suburbia also drew on the practical Central European tradition of building large apartment blocks for worker housing, as in Berlin. The two streams had combined, for example, in Vienna's Karl-Marx-Hof (1927–30), with 1,382 apartments in a building a kilometer long. Uniform buildings with identical apartments embodied the egalitarianism of socialist ideology, and as Khrushchev noted, modern construction materials and techniques made the option financially appealing for fast-growing or reconstructing cities.

Neither the old stone apartments of Prague nor the superficially fetching art deco apartments of Bucharest could house tens of thousands of newcomers each year, so socialist states dotted new apartment clusters around older cities. Back in the USSR, the typical building grew from five stories to ten or fifteen stories during the Brezhnev years (1964–81), with 80 percent of new Moscow-area housing built in standardized mass housing between 1960 and 2000. The figures were also 80 percent for Bucharest, 60 percent for Sofia, and 55 percent for Warsaw.

Apartments were small, but they were clean and modern. Standard plans might include a bedroom, living room, kitchen, bath, and entrance hall. Socialist planners borrowed the modernist neighborhood unit concept from the American Clarence Stein and amped it up for apartments rather than single-family houses. The Russian term is *mikrorayon*, or microdistrict. Each district included schools, open space, community centers, and shops within sets of apartment buildings. The ideal was community-scale clusters for a few thousand people each, but projects could be massive: Petrazalka, built across the Danube from Bratislava in the 1970s and early 1980s, has 50,000 dwelling units in more than 100 tall buildings.

Socialist high-rise suburbs were integrated with the metropolis, neither distant nor isolated. Prague had developed with three rings: core, old apartments, and middle-class houses from the interwar years. The 1960s and 1970s added a fourth ring of housing estates. They were commuter suburbs, with residents who held jobs in the city center or nearby factories. They were close enough for Bulgarian teens to take the bus into Sofia for a little fun and then complain when late-night service was infrequent.

It is no surprise that popular culture took up high-rise suburbia. For sixteen years Bratislava television aired a soap opera titled simply *Panelak*. Russian filmmakers played with the monotony of slab apartments in *The Irony of Fate, or Enjoy Your Bath!* (1976), immensely popular as a two-part television program and a recut theatrical release. After a drunken bachelor party on New Year's Eve, attendees mistakenly bundle Muscovite Zhenya on a plane to Leningrad. In his bleary state he gives his address to the taxi driver. Surprise: Leningrad has a street with the same name, an apartment building with the same address, an apartment with the same number, which he opens with the key used for apartments all over Russia—standardization in the extreme. Screwball confusion ensues until the logic of the romantic comedy takes hold and Zhenya and Nadya, the occupant of the Leningrad premises, realize they are destined to be together. The film has replayed on New Year's Eve in most of the former Warsaw Pact nations, a bit like the repetition of *It's a Wonderful Life* in the United States.

Slab housing fell on hard times with the end of state socialism, showing its age and denigrated as rabbit hutches, in the words of Vaclav Havel. Moscow *Khrushchevka* in desirable locations have been targets for demolition and redevelopment. Tenants with means moved to newer private-market housing. Other tenants, however, bought their apartments at affordable prices as postsocialist governments emulated Margaret Thatcher's "right to buy" program and got out of the public housing business. In prosperous cities, better-located apartments have become increasingly fashionable. Owners have renovated their own units (soundproofing is a priority) and upgraded common areas—cheerful Mediterranean colors improve gray concrete. The mixed fate of slab-built suburbs is not too different from that of postwar American suburbs. Some have gone downhill, some continue to serve working-class families, and some are gentrifying.

The banlieues of France

Six years after the international success of *Breathless* (1961), with its gritty depiction of central Paris, director Jean-Luc Godard turned to a very different cityscape in *Two or Three Things I Know About Her* (1967). The setting is a group of high-rise apartments known as Le Quatre Mille, located five miles northeast of the center of Paris in the commune of La Courneuve. The name refers to the 4,000 residents of the complex. Its four sterile buildings, optimistically named for French literary luminaries, including Balzac, reflect the empty life of the bourgeois residents; the word *her* in the film's title can refer to the bored wife at the center of the story, but also to capitalism, the Paris region, or oppressive architecture. Le Quatre Mille was one of many clusters of high-rise apartments that the French call *grand ensembles* or *cités*.

Several nations of Atlantic Europe tried the same approach of suburban high-rise housing. Sweden had tried out mid-rise suburban apartments built by nonprofit building societies in the 1930s, and semiutopian Vallingby expanded the concept there. Local authorities in Glasgow and Birmingham sprinkled six- and eight-story blocks of flats on the periphery in the 1950s and 1960s. Low-keyed Norwegians took advantage of Oslo's natural setting by siting modernist suburban apartment clusters in a wide valley flanked by protected forests. The ideas of the Swiss French architect Le Corbusier shaped Multifamiliar Alemán, six high-rise apartment blocks on the southern fringe of Mexico City, the city's first public housing project that served its growing middle class.

Nevertheless, Paris has captured the most attention, perhaps because it is a global media center, perhaps because people who have walked the Latin Quarter as tourists are taken aback to know that more Parisians live in peripheral apartment blocks than in quaint Montmartre, or perhaps because Paris suburbs epitomize the racial and class divides of contemporary Europe. Parisian banlieues are a mixed landscape. Single-family houses, factories, shopping centers, and commercial strips are a low-density background out of which rise the *grand ensembles* that the French government built in the 1960s and 1970s to house people drawn by the magnetic economy of the capital. The parallels to Eastern Europe are clear. The state created high-rise suburbs by acquiring peripheral land and using modern construction techniques to provide rental housing for a growing metropolis without disturbing the historic Paris cityscape.

Initial residents of the *grand ensembles* were solidly French and middle class, like Juliette Jeanson (Marina Vlady) in Godard's movie. That changed in the 1980s and 1990s. Middle-class families moved up and outward to new single-family houses, replaced by families of North African and West African heritage. Rioting by Arab-heritage youth in a working-class suburb of Lyon in 1981 presaged sporadic disorder in the 1990s, motivated by the frustrations of poverty, bias in policing, and suburban social isolation and then an explosion of rioting in 2005. The epicenter was the Paris banlieue of Clichy-sous-Bois, one of the poorest areas of the metropolis. Rioting spread to other banlieues in the northeastern suburbs and to other cities over the course of three weeks in October and November.

Banlieue technically means a peripheral zone that is administratively attached to a city. Since the 1980s, however, it has increasingly applied to lower-income districts with deteriorating high-rise housing and ethnically mixed populations. The reputation of the *grand ensembles* plunged in government circles and the media. They stand as the dark mirror for touristic Paris—ugly, uncouth, and dark skinned rather than beautiful, civilized, and French. *La Haine* (1995) is the best known of scores of banlieue films and documentaries; it sympathetically explores the tensions between suburban youth of color and the police while depicting their community as a wilderness of concrete. French publications lamented the *crise de banlieues* and adopted the analogy of the America ghetto. "Banlieues are where the worst is possible," the conservative paper *Le Figaro* wrote in 1990. Young people have internalized the negative image, telling interviewers that they live in a "chicken coop" or a "reservation." "The Quatre Mille is an insult," said one. "We take it like a slap in the face." The science fiction film *Banlieue 13* (2004) imagined a vast suburban tract walled off from the outside.

Reputation and reality are not a good match. The older banlieues remain a mix of immigrants and French nationals. Before the explosions of 2005, crime was largely youth brawls and petty theft; in 2005, rioters were much more likely to torch automobiles (in the thousands) than to assault individuals. The neighborhoods have vibrant multiethnic culture as well as crime. Nevertheless, some of the towers have been demolished in favor of new lower-density housing, a parallel to American demolition and replacement of inner-city public housing.

Across Europe, high-rise suburbs represent a response to the specific challenge of housing new urban residents as Western European nations such as France and Belgium completed the rural–urban transformation and many Eastern European nations felt the full force of the rapid change from agrarian to industrial–urban societies. Some apartment blocks have been demolished, some have become trendy, and millions of others continue to provide housing for people of modest means, while families with money have opted for new "American-style" developments with freestanding houses.

Asia's apartment suburbs

You are unlikely to go wrong if you assume that an ordinary resident of Singapore or Seoul lives in an apartment tower outside the city center. In Europe, high-rise suburbs for the middling classes were a twentieth-century expedient that is no longer the first or only choice of government policy and private developers. In many parts of Asia in the early twenty-first century, 600-foot apartment buildings were the normal tool for turning peripheral land into new communities. Although Indians use other terminology, many members of Delhi's middle class live in mid- and high-rise suburbs. The New Towns of Seoul are apartment towns; in the metropolitan region, 60 percent of the population live in high-rise apartments and another 25 percent in smaller apartment buildings. Residential towers have transformed redeveloped core districts in Seoul and Shanghai just as they have in London and Vancouver, but they also dominate the urban periphery in Asia in a way very unlike that in the United Kingdom or Canada.

Newly independent Singapore faced a housing problem in 1959. Most non-English residents of the colonial city lived in picturesque but crowded and dilapidated shophouses or growing shanty communities. If it was to thrive, the city-state needed to provide for workers and upgrade its image—remnants of the colonial past for tourists and modern housing for workers. And it needed to do so within an island that stretches thirty miles on one axis and seventeen on the other.

The solution of the People's Action Party was to convince Singaporeans that they wanted to live in new apartment towers built outside the old city. It established the Housing and Development Board in 1960 and followed with the Homeownership for the People Scheme in 1964. The Housing and Development Board built clusters of ten-story high-rises to a standard design, with the outside corridors that the tropical climate allowed. There was electricity and water in each flat and shops and playgrounds for each cluster. In contrast to Europe, the innovation was to make the flats owner-occupied housing. The government used payroll deductions to force workers to save for down payments and sold the flats on ninety-nine-year leases—a Singaporean version of the Federal Housing Administration and Veterans Administration mortgage programs with which the United States supported suburban ownership. The evolving

7. The large majority of Singapore's population lives in public housing constructed by the Housing and Development Board since the 1960s. Laundry hanging out from back verandas, as at the early Bukit Ho Swee estate, was a common sight in small Housing and Development Board flats.

program had placed increasing emphasis on dividing massive New Towns into neighborhoods and then precincts of ten buildings, each with the appropriate level of community facilities and shopping. The government added a social engineering requirement that each building have a minimum number of Chinese, Malay, and Indian households; in a nation with three major ethnic groups, avoiding ethnic enclaves was a must.

Housing and Development Board flats age well. More than a million units house 80 percent of the nation's population. Over the decades, towers have grown taller—up to fifty stories—and apartments larger. Singaporeans can now reserve a flat in a building while it is in the planning stages. Upgraded older units retain their middle-class appeal, with substantial resale value despite diminishing time on leases (one calculation estimates that the value of a three-room apartment has increased twentyfold since the 1970s). Tourists in Singapore can see some of the newest towers on the road from Changi Airport to its world-city core, but they are less likely to ride the city's excellent trains five or eight miles out to see how millions of everyday citizens live beyond the glamorous Singapore of *Crazy Rich Asians*.

The suburban remaking of postcolonial Singapore is impressive, but the transformation of Chinese cities can be overwhelming. Maoist-era cities were compact with a distinct urban–rural boundary and housing for specific work units (*danwei*) built adjacent to workplaces. Economic liberalization created a private real estate development sector that looked to cheap peripheral land for commodity housing. The market has operated on multiple tracks, with private builders, local governments, and rural communes all seeking to meet intense housing demand with profitable development. Municipalities controlled extensive territories that allowed them to partner with developers to put up islands of suburban housing that have grown into high-rise continents served by new highways in a much denser version of the North American freeway–housing symbiosis.

China's new suburbs range from luxurious to basic. Walled estates for the upper crust have amenities like banquet halls and fitness centers and are run by professional management companies. They are often marketed with the cachet of European or American lifestyle. In contrast, families struggling to make it into the middle class can find unadorned apartments in six-story walk-up buildings in rural townships, which are legally the collective owners of their agricultural land. The legal status of the apartments is ambiguous, but their construction benefits township members and meets a real need for people who cannot afford new market-built apartments or find housing closer to the city center.

Let's take another look at Beijing, where suburbanization has moved outward to the third, fourth, and fifth ring roads. Wangjing, for example, lies just inside the fifth ring road on the way to the Beijing Capital International Airport. In 1980, the area was farmland dotted with factories and *danwei* housing in Soviet-style apartments. In the early twenty-first century it is a well-established suburb. Two-income families of government workers, teachers, and middle managers fill some of the new towers, and employees of international companies could afford the more luxurious apartments with big windows, nice appointments, and surrounding green space. There is a new subway, but many families have their own cars. The most successful have been described as "citizens of modernity" who participate in the global economy, pursue an affluent lifestyle, and, at least in the early 2000s, obsess about real estate.

New Beijing suburbanites evaluate their new homes from their class perspective. New suburbanites with limited incomes respond not too differently than the first residents of British New Towns did. People who had been displaced from their traditional Beijing *hutong* to a suburban tower to clear inner-city land for the 2004 Olympics admitted that the apartment was more modern and comfortable than what they left behind, but older people in particular missed chatting with their friends at the corner shop. In contrast, the anonymity of new apartment living did not bother a younger generation who saw up-to-date Wangjing as a good place for young people, even if it meant juggling journeys among multiple locations for workplaces, schools, and shopping.

There is a continuum from suburbs with a scattering of high-rises to peripheral districts consisting almost exclusively of apartment towers. A single condominium tower stands in the center of McLean, Virginia, a community that is otherwise quintessential American suburbia. High-rise apartments are easy to spot on the drive from central Toronto to Pearson Airport. In the United Kingdom, Birmingham scattered several dozen apartment towers on the city's outskirts in the council housing era of the 1950s and 1960s. Newer high-rise housing can be found in major transit modes like New Westminster, fifteen miles from Vancouver. Along the south beaches of Rio de Janeiro twenty-five miles from the city, the ocean side of Barra de Tijuca is lined with towering apartments for the rich. In all these cities, however, most folks live in low-rise housing.

Bucharest, Bratislava, and Beijing are different, cities where peripheral apartment towers were, or are, the primary option for new suburban housing. Vertical suburbs do not look like bourgeois utopias such as Brookline, Massachusetts, or Scarsdale, New York; a garden suburb like Letchworth or Radburn; or the everyday American landscape of low-slung houses, two-story apartments, and strip malls. Nevertheless, they have served the same function by transforming land on city peripheries to affordable housing for tens of millions of new city people.

Chapter 4

Improvised suburbs

The Italian film director Vittorio De Sica was known for gritty realism, but he employed a lighter touch with *Il Tetto (The Roof)* in 1956. The movie is the story of newlyweds who are fed up with living with the wife's parents and strike off on their own. They find an unused piece of land and start to build. They have only one night to get a door and roof on their new house. If they manage, they cannot be evicted, even though they have built on railroad property and without proper permits.

Improvised or do-it-yourself housing is one of the ways that suburbs get built. Affluent twenty-first-century folks in the Global North are likely to understand improvised suburbs as a phenomenon of shantytowns and vast peripheral slums in the Global South. In fact, people turn to irregular do-it-yourself housing out of necessity in any circumstance where neither government construction of public housing nor the formal housing market can keep up with demand—Italy in the early 1950s as well as Nairobi in the 2010s.

Improvised suburbs vary widely in appearance and physical character from one nation and decade to another, but they share two overlapping characteristics. One is that they are in some way irregular or informal (better terms than illegal). Residents may lack title to the land on which they build, even if they pick land for which there is no immediate market demand. They may have title, but build in areas that are not formally zoned or designated for housing, and the structures they erect may not meet minimum building codes. The second is that they are built with minimal or no involvement of the professional construction industry. The builders are family members and neighbors, not professional tradespeople. The materials they use may be scavenged or substandard. We can use different terms, including self-built, self-help, owner-built, autoconstructed, and incremental, but the implications are similar whatever the terminology.

Self-built suburbs in industrial cities

Working-class families in the early twentieth century could not afford nicely planned suburbs with curving streets, but they could buy a cheap lot among the factories of the industrial fringe of growing cities and build their own houses bit by bit to create self-built suburbs—a pattern as true for Buenos Aires as for Toronto. From the outside, such self-built neighborhoods were disheveled and disreputable. The pioneering photographer Eugène Atget traveled to the fringe of Paris to photograph a ragpicker's hut, and a French commentator in 1922 described owner-built worker housing outside Paris as "a low structure, insufficiently dimensioned . . . everything constructed of light materials, infinitely varied and often of the most unexpected sort." It probably did not help that low-status suburbs were developing a reputation as the city's Red Belt of socialist voters. Working-class households could have a different idea. Chagrin Falls Park was a small African American suburb outside Cleveland. Outsiders called it a shantytown and a "curse." Residents took pride in their community and remembered hardworking early days; as Ruby Hall recalled, "The neighbors dug the basement by hand and my father and another man that lived down the street built the house."

The story was similar for many families who sought work in booming Los Angeles. South Gate, Bell Gardens, and Home

Gardens were among many working-class suburbs that grew in the early twentieth century around new suburban industry, in this case a manufacturing district southeast of the city center. The latter echoed Chicago's S. E. Gross from decades earlier; it was "where the workingman is welcomed and given an even break." Lots were large and cheap, with space for families to live while they built their own house while self-provisioning with chicken coops, rabbit hutches, gardens, and fruit trees. South Gate explicitly allowed families to live in tents and garages while working on their houses. Juanita Hammon recalled,

> My dad was a good builder, and he had help. My mother was just as good a carpenter as he was. She laid hardwood floors and kept up with him....She helped nail those floors in, and with a lot of things. And all us kids helped. We'd hold a board while my dad was sawing, or we would climb up to take supplies to him, or help hold something. I know I climbed up that ladder many times to take him some more nails or a certain piece of wood he wanted. We all helped build that house.

Elsewhere in the Los Angeles basin, labor camps for Mexican American farm and railroad workers evolved in the 1910s, 1920s, and 1930s into permanent *colonias* for year-round citrus workers. Segregated Latino neighborhoods developed on the outskirts of towns like Pacoima and El Monte. As of 1920, Riverside's 500 African Americans and 1,000 Mexicans lived only on the east side of town. Real estate developers marketed explicitly to Mexicans, selling small frame houses or bare lots where worker families could put up tents and build for themselves. The Anaheim Chamber of Commerce encouraged subdividers to market to Mexicans because owners of even the most modest homes would be a permanent labor supply. In the northern half of Orange County alone there were at least a dozen and a half *colonias* in 1940, clustered around La Habra, Placentia, Yorba Linda, Garden Grove, and Santa Ana. The latter city had only 12 Mexican families in 1900 but 4,000 Mexican residents by 1930, living in the *colonias* of Delhi, Logan, and Artesia. Hardscrabble and partly self-built though they may have been, farm-fringe streetcar suburbs developed a rich community life of baseball teams, churches, and celebrations.

Los Angeles was not unusual. Perhaps one-third of new housing in Detroit, Milwaukee, and Toronto was also self-built in the first two decades of the twentieth century. The formula: start with a shed or garage to live in while building a small house from scrounged lumber, used fixtures, and tarpaper. On Chicago's fringes were African Americans in Robbins, Hungarians in South Chicago, and Poles in Stone Park—the latter described on the so-called redlining maps of the federal Home Owners' Loan Corporation maps as a place of "indiscriminate owner-built shacks." Toronto's do-it-yourself neighborhoods had a thirty-year run. Industrialists in search of cheap land and low taxes moved factories beyond the eastern city limits, and workers followed. The *Toronto Sunday World* in 1909 ran a headline: "High Rents in City Force Many People to Build Their Own Homes on City Outskirts." Thirty to thirty-five percent of new dwellings in the Toronto area from 1901 to 1913 were built by their owners on land beyond the reach of zoning and building codes. As in Los Angeles, houses grew over time, but it was hard to shake a reputation as "shacktown, the camp of English immigrants." The Great Depression hit "shacktown" hard, idling factories and pushing workers back to the inner city and the casual labor market.

Artists have been well aware of scruffy edges. The Canadian painter Lawren Harris depicted self-built Toronto housing in a sort of suburban equivalent of the Ashcan school. John Steinbeck's Monterey, California, had "Tortilla Flat," the suburban fringe "where the streets are innocent of asphalt and the corners free of streetlights, and the old inhabitants of Monterey...live in old wooden houses set in weedy yards." Richard Hugo's poems returned repeatedly to his 1920s childhood in the Duwamish River neighborhoods on Seattle's industrial south side. The

8. French photographer Eugène Atget made a series of iconic images that captured the downside of Paris before World War I. This family of nine lived in a single-room shanty on the outskirts of the city, a reminder that new suburbs in the streetcar era were interspersed with shacks and self-built housing for the very poor.

narrator in his poem "What Thou Lovest Well, Remains American" describes a remembered cityscape of vacant lots overplatted in the 1930s, unpaved streets, and roses grown wild among scattered shacks—overgrown, ill-defined lots and shacks that feature as well in "Between the Bridges" and "West Marginal Way."

Improvised housing in North American cities is not a thing of the past, although it has increasingly taken the form of an unpermitted conversion of a garage or basement into a small apartment rather than a new stand-alone structure. The house we bought in Norfolk, Virginia, in 1972 had been patriotically divided into upstairs and downstairs apartments to meet housing demand during World War II (we did not keep the bathtub in the kitchen).

In tight Long Island or Los Angeles housing markets, unregulated conversions serve undocumented immigrants. When similar conversions are done to code by middle-class homeowners, they are auxiliary dwelling units and applauded as environmentally friendly infill.

Do-it-yourself explosion

The explosive urbanization that has transformed Latin America, Africa, and South Asia since the 1950s has really been explosive suburbanization. Rural migrants to the metropolis have often gone directly to peripheral areas where free or extremely cheap land is available and proceeded to make their own housing. Forgetting that many working-class families in the United States, Canada, Australia, and France had done the same, Western commentators in the 1950s and 1960s took a dim view of these "belts of misery" and "suburbs of despair." The author of the lead article on *Scientific American*'s special issue on cities in September 1965 bemoaned Venezuela's "thousands of squatters living in junk houses on land that does not belong to them" and extended the indictment around the world. In fact, 60 percent of Caracas housing, 50 percent in Mexico City, and 25 percent in Lima and Rio de Janeiro was self-help in the 1980s. Four decades later, well-received books about "shadow cities" (2004) and a "planet of slums" (2005) updated the argument. Such generalizations identify real problems with shelter and services. They also miss the particular patterns and histories of different countries, and they underestimate the ways in which improvised squatter settlements mature into stable communities.

Irregular suburbanization in the Global South can be daunting to approach. As in Toronto, peripheral industry attracted workers and unofficial housing. In 1990 the World Resources Institute estimated that 42 percent of the Third World urban population lived in informal settlements, most on the fringe. Mike Davis wrote about what he termed megaslums, and journalists tend to visit especially large communities on the outskirts of cities like Mumbai and Lusaka. Many such settlements are small and scattered, however, with more than 200 around Bogotá. Nor are all their residents a marginal underclass. In Rio de Janeiro and Santiago, many have grown along industrial corridors, just as in Paris, Los Angeles, and Toronto in an earlier era.

Names are telling. Moroccans began to build *bidonvilles* ("tin can towns") on the outskirts of French-ruled Casablanca in the 1920s. The French novelist Pierre Mac Orlan described "Bidonville...capital of 'abject poverty,' made of oil drums and corrugated iron." The term spread to improvised housing throughout French North Africa and then crossed the Mediterranean with North African immigrants. Migrants to Istanbul's improvised suburbs built *gecekondu*, meaning "built overnight" or "overnight settlement," recalling the plot of *Il Tetto*. The improvised communities around mid-century Buenos Aires are *villas miseria* (towns of misery). Those adjacent to the desert around Lima were *barriadas* until the government started calling them *pueblos jovenes* or "young towns," implying that they are in the process of growing into something more formal and permanent.

Peruvians are onto something. Do-it-yourself suburbs are not static. Families may live in a shack while starting work on a more substantial house to which they add rooms and even entire floors as time and money allow; the process is similar to North Americans living in an RV on a country lot while working on a stick-built house. As individual households improve their dwellings, government slowly extends services like water and sewer lines. What looks like a ragged shantytown in one decade can often be an established community in another.

Just as in Eastern Europe, the push and pull of rural poverty and urban industrialization sent millions of Spaniards and Italians toward Madrid and Rome in the 1950s and 1960s. The difference was that national governments and private investors struggled to provide standard housing, leaving many migrants to fend for themselves on unplanned, poorly serviced, and unauthorized sites tucked amid and beyond standard development. Their housing was improvised, precarious, marginally legal, and sometimes called *casas de lata* for tin-box houses. Madrileños talked about *chabola* districts, from a working-class Spanish word for shack. Dictator Francisco Franco hated them as hotbeds of left-wing agitation. Conservative Italians had the same apprehension about the residents of the illegal city that accounted for a third of new housing around Rome from 1951 to 1981. It took the rest of the century to build an adequate stock of standard housing.

Informal settlements may become a permanent part of a metropolis, but their sometimes ramshackle character does not. Residents who start with a tin can house or mud hut do not stop there, any more than the pioneers of South Gate were satisfied to sleep year after year in their garages. When any sort of regular income is available, one-room families add second rooms, tap electric lines, and otherwise make owner building an active endeavor, as with *gecekondu* in Istanbul. Rural in-migrants in the 1950s and 1960s found vacant or state-owned land where they found someone to pour a concrete slab for a shelter of concrete blocks and metal roof—no permits involved. By the early 1980s, roughly half of Istanbul's three million people lived in self-built housing, often clustered by villages and regions of origin. And they were people who kept building, installing indoor plumbing when they could, adding a new room or even a second floor. Individual investment in turn attracted outside developers to add apartments and shops. Many improvised neighborhoods of the 1970s have evolved into the suburbs of the 2020s.

One of the most familiar terms for improvised settlements is Brazil's *favela*. The word dates to 1897, when veterans of Brazil's civil war claimed a hill in central Rio de Janeiro for their own and named it Morro de Favela, after a plant common in the northeastern region where they had fought; it became a generic term when other unofficial neighborhoods popped up. Favelas grew on the city's outskirts in the same way as irregular settlements around other Latin American cities, especially on the industrial lowlands on the north side, but Rio's complex, hilly topography means that many others have dotted "unbuildable" hillsides close to the city center and upscale districts. Government policy has varied from wholesale land clearance, to formal recognition that residents cannot be evicted without replacement housing, to programs that formally inventory and define favelas to push their fuller articulation with the city as regular neighborhoods.

Viewers of the film *City of God* (2002) may think it is set in a favela. In fact, the opposite is true. The real Cidade de Deus was a Brazilian government project for people displaced by clearance of a central favela, moving them to five-story apartments and several thousand 375-square-foot houses. The film makes clear that many initial residents were not happy to be there. A resident of a similar housing project on the northern edge of Rio told a researcher that he was living at the end of the world.

Favelas come in many variations, with distinct histories and identities: "every ravine is a nation," as one song lyric puts it. *A Ten-Year Urban Plan for Rio de Janeiro* (1982) defined favela as "a predominantly residential area, occupied by low-income groups, with poor infrastructure and public services, narrow, irregular streets, land lots of irregular shapes and sizes, and unlicensed constructions in breach of legal standards." A common theme has been constant change. Houses are repeatedly modified and upgraded. Residents start businesses and accumulate capital for reinvestment, and *slum* is not an appropriate synonym despite translation site suggestions. A favela like Rocinha—the largest in Rio—has evolved from small wooden buildings on a steep hillside with no water and stolen electricity to a bustling urban neighborhood of two- to four-story concrete and brick houses and apartments that are often quite stylish. Indeed, a common theme has been constant physical change and partial but not complete incorporation into the formal city.

Making the irregular regular

Democratic governments will displace thousands or tens of thousands of citizens from valuable city land in the name of urban redevelopment, but they are reluctant to remove hundreds of thousands of voters who happen to live in self-built communities on the urban fringe. Nor are they unhappy that squatters have borne much of the initial cost of housing themselves. Engineers might decide to run a new highway through an informal settlement, but the costs of removing people on a large scale are simply too high. When local activists and politicians organize shantytown residents as voting blocs, the costs are even higher. Confronted with these circumstances, governments faced with irregular settlements have preferred to accept and regularize them when possible, which can mean granting formal land title, recognizing de facto title, and ignoring dwellings built in violation of land use zoning and building codes.

The simplest way to make irregular suburbs more regular is to extend utilities. In Guayaquil on the coast of Ecuador, migrants colonized swampy mud flats with shacks and small houses on stilts and pilings, connected by raised walkways. The government would come in with fill to level up direct roads, which made it possible to pipe in water. Residents and the authorities went through the cycle one time after another. Regularization through services has been an unsurprising demand of Brazilians in incremental settlements who have mobilized politically. In a variation in Bogotá, residents of *barriadas piratas* (pirate towns) bought land from legal owners but the government withheld formal title until they secured utility services.

It is also vital to ensure that households are secure in both *where* and *what*—that they have assurance that they can continue to live where they have built and that they will not be forced to tear it down as being substandard. Confronted with waves of rural in-migrants and burgeoning *gecekondu* districts, the Turkish government went with the flow. Repeated amnesties recognized squatter neighborhoods built before 1953, then 1966, then 1984, then 1990 as legal even though they were irregular. Householders who were grandfathered in gained enough security to enlarge or replace initial houses, although a cost of formal legal visibility is more taxes. Turkish law also allows the government to acknowledge an informal settlement as a semi-independent municipality with some taxing authority for investment in roads and services; some squatter settlements are now bustling suburban cities.

A variation is a legally unrecognized but locally accepted community property regime. Land ownership is not recorded and acknowledged by central authorities. Instead, residents in a particular settlement recognize each other's squatters' rights, as in some of the favelas of Rio. Stable settlements may develop a local real estate market. In one informal suburb north of Lima, community leaders have sold vacant lots to newcomers to raise money for community needs, somewhat like an American homeowners' association or like Ebenezer Howard's vision of Garden Cities that would benefit as a whole from rising land values. One advantage is that locals recognize each other's rights, but their community is impervious to outside speculation. At the same time, the system in some places may function more as a land mafia than as a cooperative.

Another variety of informality involves residents with legal land tenure who build without paying attention to official regulations. Brazilian *loteamentos irregulares* (irregular allotments) are suburbs where land has been legally acquired by a subdivider who lays out streets, sells building plots, perhaps without recording the transfer, and provides minimal services. The subdivisions may be on the far urban fringe on barren, unappealing land, but that is why the lots can be cheap. In São Paulo, 80 percent of self-builders have legitimate claims to property ownership. As with similar situations in Mexico and Peru, residents can organize as homeowners to gain recognition and services that make them a more "regular" part of the city.

An additional way to regularize autoconstruction is through aided self-help, an approach that American consultants developed out of initial experiences in Puerto Rico. National governments and/or international aid agencies would provide plans, materials, and funds to leverage individual household labor in constructing or completing new housing. Getting households involved in the building process leverages an "underutilized" resource of household labor at low capital investment. Tied directly to ownership, it also gave poorly housed working-class households a stake in stable society. Aided self-help had the approval of the Organization of American States, becoming a key element in US foreign aid in Latin America, to a lesser extent in Africa, and later in United Nations and World Bank programs.

The government of Colombia made aided self-help a basic housing policy. In Bogota, Ciudad Kennedy was built in part with American aid. It was a showpiece for the Alliance for Progress, the Kennedy administration program to build good relations with Latin America through economic development assistance. On cheap fringe land the government built bare shells, supplied building materials, and sold the houses with affordable fifteen-year mortgages. The occupants tended to be skilled workers and government employees with an inside track. As they finished the homes, some ran side businesses or took in renters. They liked what they had, even with an inconvenient location, and many became long-term and satisfied residents. A survey found that they valued having a roof in old age, no rent to pay, independence, and something to leave to their children.

At worst, self-built communities remain substandard in both housing and services. At best, they are architecture that works, especially as rural to urban migration has slowed in much of the Global South. In the positive case, the trajectory is similar in many parts of the world. Housing embodies hope for the future, and family and house evolve together. Housing also embodies status, prompting self-builders outside São Paulo to build an attractive face and front entrance before finishing the more functional parts. Colombia's National Planning Office in 1974 described the evolution of Bogotá's self-built suburbs:

> A simple unplanned solution served for a time in Colombia of providing a site (or acquiescence in the illegal acquisition of a site unlicensed for building) and permitting the owner to build as, how, and when he could, and providing services later in one way or another. In the course of time many such neighborhoods which started out as ramshackle and unsanitary slums became acceptable barrios and the original occupants built up a patrimony....A sense of neighborhood was preserved, and services gradually improved...most such building has occurred in pirate neighborhoods [*barrios piratas*].

Chapter 5
Suburban work

Henry Ford housed his first automobile assembly operations in a converted wagon shop on Mack Avenue in Detroit and then in a small factory on Piquette Avenue, about two miles from the city center. When the automobile industry and his own fortunes took off, he went big and moved outward in 1909, building a factory for Model Ts on 102 acres in the inner suburb of Highland Park. A decade later, the Ford Motor Company was again on the move, this time to suburban Dearborn, to build its headquarters, research department, and the massive River Rouge plant. At the time the world's largest vertically integrated industrial complex, it extended 1.5 miles along the dredged river and had its own generating plant, steel mill, and millions of square feet of factory space. The plant became an icon of American industry, photographed and painted by Charles Sheeler and inspiring Diego Rivera's fabulous *Detroit Industry* murals in the Detroit Institute of Arts.

Two generations later, in an Albuquerque, New Mexico, strip mall, Bill Gates and Paul Allen started a company that Allen named Microsoft. Their next-door neighbor was a vacuum cleaner repair shop. After three years they moved the growing company "home," but to suburban Bellevue rather than the Seattle neighborhoods where they had grown up. Microsoft has ever since been a suburban company, now with a 500-acre campus of unassuming office buildings in Redmond, Washington, half the size of the River Rouge site and far less photogenic, but just as central to the world economy.

The eras and industrial categories are different, but the takeaway is the same—the suburbs have long been places where work happens. The 1950s and 1960s gave Americans the image of the employed suburbanite as the man in the gray flannel suit who took the train on the daily commute to his city office. His English counterpart wore a bowler hat and carried an umbrella. In reality, both the industrial economy and the so-called postindustrial economy have been substantially suburban. Workers have long built things out of wood and metal in suburban factories, just as more recent tech workers write code in their own suburban production centers.

Industrial sprawl

Henry Ford was an innovator in marketing automobiles, but he followed the crowd in choosing sites for his factories. Over the half century before the Model T hit the road, technologies of production had gradually changed the character of manufacturing. The cotton mills that crowded the center of 1830s Manchester, England, used stationary steam engines that delivered power to machinery on multiple overhead levels with belt and pulley systems. The availability of electric power by the end of the nineteenth century, in contrast, allowed machinery to be sited laterally in production lines; the modern factory spread its floor area horizontally rather than vertically. Railroads helped to decentralize manufacturing just as they decentralized housing by giving access to inexpensive land for new horizontal factories and warehouses and making it easy to ship output.

The new locational dynamics sorted manufacturing into two clusters. Industries that relied on small-batch production for multiple clients tended to remain in city centers—hence inner-city garment districts and printers' rows. In contrast, companies that produced standardized durable goods had incentives to move to sites where they could spread out. Paris factory owners found sites north and south of the city. London industry extended the crowded East End farther east; in 1931, Ford cloned River Rouge by opening a massive operation at Dagenham on the Thames downstream from London. A special suburban attraction in North America was escape from city taxes and building regulations, an important factor in persuading Toronto business owners to build factories beyond the city's eastern boundary. The ability to dominate the politics of governmentally separate suburban municipalities served the interests of industrialists in Milwaukee (West Allis, Cudahy), Buffalo (Lackawanna, Tonawanda), St. Louis (Granite City, East St. Louis), Chicago (Cicero, Melrose Park), and Pittsburgh (McKeesport, Braddock), as well as Detroit.

Factory districts in Montreal extended both east along the St. Lawrence River and west along the Lachine Canal, which bypassed a set of rapids. The process unfolded from the mid-nineteenth century into the twentieth century; as the city engulfed older districts, industrialists built newer factories farther out. Montréal-Est had cement plants and oil refineries. Maisonneuve developed with model housing for workers and the aspiration to be the Pittsburgh of Canada. It was a common pattern for river cities where suburbanizing industry could utilize both water and riverside rail transportation.

Los Angeles manufacturing was suburban from the start. In the 1910s, Jared Torrance purchased thousands of acres of agricultural land along two railroad lines between downtown Los Angeles and its port at San Pedro. He offered prime sites for companies producing heavy equipment and automobile equipment while hiring Frederick Law Olmsted Jr. to plan the residential districts and community center. Nonindustrial Torrance was attractive (the high school stood in for West Beverly High School in *Beverly Hills 90210* and Sunnydale High in *Buffy the Vampire Slayer*).

However, its industrial base replicated in a dozen other suburbs where factories served the growing California consumer market and exploited the rich oil fields south of the city. The filmmakers moved to Burbank and Culver City to build warehouses and sound stages. The postwar aerospace industry was suburban from the start; iconic Los Angeles suburbs like Westminster and Lakewood developed in tandem with the aerospace industry.

The same reformers who celebrated garden suburbs also saw suburban factories as the solution to industrial blight. The planning propaganda film *The City* drew a contrast between reeking, smoke-choked Pittsburgh and clean new factories. Halfway through, it cuts from crowded city scenes to show a DC-3 cruising above Hoover Dam. The film was made at the height of American enthusiasm for hydroelectric power, notably huge dam projects on the Tennessee and Columbia Rivers, and the narrator extols the virtues of electric power as the plane flies eastward. The next scene shows workers leaving a bright, low-slung factory nestled in greenery, headed home to scenes shot in Greenbelt, Maryland. Every economic development agency for the past three generations that has pursued "clean" electronics, pharmaceutical, and other supposedly clean companies and every suburban industrial park with one-floor flex space built with tilt-up panels has been following the same script.

Company suburbs and industrial satellites

George Pullman discovered that it was hard to be a benevolent capitalist, especially when you knew what was right for your workers. In the 1880s, his Pullman Palace Car Company was the equivalent of Airbus or Boeing in the early twenty-first century. It manufactured and operated the sleeping cars that made long-distance rail travel comfortable. Pullman was a hard-driving entrepreneur who built a new factory for manufacturing and repairing his sleeping cars on Chicago's far south side. Because it was the middle of nowhere among marshes and sloughs, he also built housing for his workers. He was active in Chicago civic organizations such as the YMCA and concerned about the health and morality of the laboring classes. He believed that it was in the employer's interest to see that workers were "clean, contented, sober, educated, and happy." He hoped that a fully planned and complete community would benefit everyone, providing a stable workforce while "ennobling and refining" them.

Pullman built the factory, community facilities from schools and churches to a retail arcade, and housing—detached and semidetached houses for managers, small apartments for families, and three-story tenements for unmarried workers. "Baleful influences" were to be banished. The only place to buy a beer was the hotel bar for visiting businessmen. Workers who wanted a drink had to trek across a buffer of empty land to an adjacent settlement. Pullman wanted to shape upstanding citizens with "habits of respectability." Thousands of visitors to the Chicago World's Fair of 1893 took an excursion to admire the quality of the houses, which had piped water on every floor, the upkeep of the common areas, and the generally tidy appearance of the town. They saw a company suburb where "all that is ugly, discordant and demoralizing is eliminated and all that insures to self-respect to thrift and to cleanliness of thought is generously provided." It was not that the company inquired deeply into the personal lives of workers and their families. Economist Richard Ely was one of the few who saw Pullman's reality: "The power of Bismarck in Germany is utterly insignificant when compared with the power of the ruling authority of the Pullman Palace Car Company in Pullman....It is benevolent, well-wishing feudalism, which desires the happiness of the people, but in such a way as well pleased the authorities."

The social experiment could not outlast labor strife. The economic depression that hit in 1893–94 caused Pullman to cut wages without cutting rents, although it allowed a rent moratorium. A strike by Pullman workers led to near paralysis of the nation's economy as other railroad workers joined in, prompting President Grover Cleveland to dispatch federal troops. Pullman hired back strikers if they forswore future union membership. The company prospered, but not the reputation of the town. In 1898 the Illinois Supreme Court ordered the Palace Car Company to divest itself of all its nonindustrial property. In the third decade of the twenty-first century, the town is a somewhat gentrified and nationally recognized historic district.

British industrialists certainly knew about the praise of Pullman and the problems that ran it off the rails. George Cadbury and William Lever were both better at benevolence than righteous, rigid George Pullman. Lever was a successful soap manufacturer who built a new factory on the Mersey River opposite Liverpool, accompanied by a model town for his workers. Port Sunlight, named for his successful packaged laundry detergent, had much in common with Pullman, including Lever's firm conviction that he knew best and had control over the housing. However, the company avoided labor strife and steadily added to community amenities. George Cadbury, Quaker and chocolate king, ran a giant corporation and bought himself very nice houses. In 1893 he also created a model community for the workers at his factory on the south side of Birmingham. The purpose of Bournville was to "ameliorate the condition of the working-class and labouring population... by the provision of improved dwellings, with gardens and open space to be enjoyed therewith." He invested in such community amenities as a large playing ground for men and a less public one for women. Houses were available at prices that skilled workers and technicians could afford. Cadbury wanted to control how the community developed, but did not see it as a source of profit; in 1900 he transferred the community to a Bournville Village Trust that has continued to expand and develop the community. A century later, BBC News asked, "Is this the nicest place to live in Britain?" and the answer was a qualified yes—nice and neighborly, but a bit stodgy and still with no pubs.

United States Steel went Pullman one better. The giant conglomerate organized on the foundation of Andrew Carnegie's steel company decided it needed a new steel mill on the southern end of Lake Michigan, where iron ore arriving by lake freighter from Minnesota could meet coal trains from Pennsylvania and West Virginia. Pullman was fifteen miles from the Chicago Loop, and Gary, Indiana, named for the company's founding chairman, was thirty miles away. The site was a washboard of sand dunes and marshes, leveled to a uniform plane in 1905 and 1906 to accommodate a grid not very different from speculative town plans of the nineteenth century. The company dredged a new harbor for its steel mill and left it up to workers to buy lots and build their own houses on the other side of the Wabash Railroad tracks. The company's only control was to withhold land title until the house was complete. Within a decade it had twice as many people as Pullman and would top out at 175,000 in 1970 before deindustrialization hit.

U.S. Steel's original ambition was for Gary to be the first of a string of industrial satellites marching along the lakeshore toward Chicago. The scheme anticipated early Soviet schemes for a linear industrial metropolis strung along railroad lines. It did not quite work out, but other corporations and developers filled out a twenty-mile corridor of suburban steel plants, oil refineries, tank farms, and factories that long dominated the southeastern entry to Chicago.

Forty years after U.S. Steel built Gary, Poland built a socialist counterpart with Nowa Huta (New Steelworks). The southern Polish city of Kracow was heavily Catholic, conservative, and not always enthusiastic about communism. As a counterbalance, the government in 1948 picked a site seven miles to the east to serve the Vladimir Lenin Steelworks. Gary was low-rise and nondescript. Nowa Huta was a socialist showcase with a classically symmetrical street plan, wide boulevards and parks, and apartment blocks with elegant facades. With street names like

Avenue of the Shock Workers and Six-Year Plan Avenue, it was "the pride of our nation" and "the forge of prosperity." The socialist leadership intended it not as a satellite, but as half of a double-star system in which old and new cities revolved around each other. In the early twenty-first century it is a district of greater Krakow, just as Gary is part of the Chicago metropolitan area.

Nowa Huta spanned two categories of town planning. It resembled industrial colonies, cities created beyond the shadow of existing cities to utilize natural resources, such as Longview, Washington (lumber mills); Kitmat, British Columbia (aluminum smelter); and Ciudad Guyana, Venezuela (hydroelectric power). Magnitogorsk, a huge steel mill city that the Soviet Union built in the 1930s, was an especially strong model for postwar Eastern Europe. It was also another postwar European New Town, many of which Polish planners had carefully studied in the 1950s and 1960s.

Edgeless cities and edge cities

On the east side of Portland, Oregon, 82nd Avenue marks a rough divide between prewar and postwar urbanization. It is an ungainly street of small, low-rise retail and parking lots flanking four lanes of traffic. It is also a very useful part of the metropolitan economy. You will find gas stations, affordable motels, auto glass repair shops, used car lots, tire stores, discount appliance stores, and lots of fast food; you will also find a failed shopping mall converted to a community college job training center and a cluster of Asian businesses that promote themselves as the new Chinatown. Some years back I bought a small pickup and needed to install a canopy to keep my golden retrievers safe and dry on drives to Mount Hood. That product was not available in the trendier commercial districts closer to my house. Instead, I drove to 82nd and had the choice of three businesses that could fabricate either vinyl or aluminum to fit my truck. The street is not pretty—some might call it an epitome of ugly sprawl—but it fills a niche in the metropolitan economy. After all, nobody is likely to order a pickup canopy online, nor are Chinese American community leaders likely to get together over dim sum delivered by Uber Eats.

This street and its many thousand siblings and cousins are parts of the "edgeless" city where millions of Americans earn their paychecks. The majority of North American suburban employment is neither in edge cities nor in Silicon thises-and-thats, but rather in scattered building supply showrooms and warehouses, low-rise office parks, big-box retailers, Amazon distribution centers, and strip malls housing insurance agents, used-book stores, Thai restaurants, and fitness clubs. Occasional mid-rise office buildings provide space for financial advisors and accountants who want to make a good impression.

This commercial landscape serves the residents of single-family neighborhoods and the tenants of millions of suburban low-rise suburban apartments as well as single-family houses. Along a major arterial will be a strip mall, perhaps with a multiscreen movie theater. Nearby will be sets of two-story "garden apartments" facing interior parking and flanked by blocks of modest houses. The whole unofficial and unplanned neighborhood may have 4,000 residents at urban density but with a suburban feel. Copy and paste dozens of times across the metropolis to describe a common suburbscape. It is the environment that Richard Ford captured in *Independence Day* (2001), a novel about a real estate salesman during the Reagan years whose territory includes a chunk of suburban New Jersey, somewhere between Princeton and New Brunswick. Here are subdivisions backed up to a minimum-security prison for white-collar criminals; a declining mall with a Cinema XII; a small town engulfed by suburbia where the town offices have been moved into a mini-mall along Route 1; a condo development that never quite caught on, next to a strip mall with medical offices and fast-food joints.

Interspersed in the scattered retail landscape are the planned shopping centers familiar to every North American. Their distant ancestor is the shopping center that J. C. Nichols built for his Country Club district in Kansas City, where automobile parking was placed in front of a row of shops. The key design innovations came in the early 1950s. Seattle's Northgate Mall (1950) imitated a downtown street by running an inward-facing corridor of shops between anchor department stores at each end, surrounded by parking. Southdale in Minneapolis (1955) added a roof for weather protection and climate control. Planned malls proliferated. Real estate professionals divided them by size: community, regional, and superregional serving successively larger markets. The 1990s were the apogee of mallworld, with the Mall of America outside Minneapolis (1992) the largest in the United States and the West Edmonton Mall (1982–99) the largest on the continent, with 800 shops and restaurants. Malls were entertainment centers and social centers for teens and the elderly.

9. The enclosed multilevel shopping mall was an American innovation in the 1950s. It scaled up older enclosed arcades such as Galleria Vittorio Emanuele II in Milan for post–World War II consumers. In turn, the enclosed mall has been adopted across the affluent nations of Asia and Europe, as with the Oberoi Mall in the Goregaon district of Mumbai.

As in the competition to build the tallest skyscraper, Asia took the lead in the shopping center race in the twenty-first century. For megamalls that match or surpass West Edmonton, head to Greater Manila, Kuala Lumpur, Dubai, and Beijing's fourth and fifth ring roads. Fickle North Americans meanwhile have turned to big-box retailers, sometimes grouped in "power centers" or sets of separate boxes that float like icebergs in seas of parking, and to online shopping with home delivery—a trend that accelerated as people stayed home to avoid COVID-19 and that is yet to reach saturation. Home delivery has exacerbated an existing problem of overbuilding, leaving suburbs to come up with plans for repurposing derelict Kmarts and half-empty malls.

Here and there the commercial fabric thickens even more, like a few random snowballs being rolled back and forth until they turn into a snowman. In 1991, journalist Joel Garreau coined the term *edge city* for large clumps of retail and office space that jut vertically above their suburban surroundings. Districts like Tyson's Corner, Virginia, outside Washington, and Galleria–Post Oak in Houston are described as destinations in their own right and full alternatives to old downtowns. As places of production and consumption, they are a capitalist opposite of Soviet bloc apartment clusters. They coalesce at key beltway exits and commuter rail stops and sometimes around airports like Chicago's O'Hare or John Wayne Airport in Orange County, California, causing enthusiastic urbanists to talk about the rise of the aerotropolis. The nomenclature—edge city, outer city, technoburb—seems to imply that these centers are more "urban" than suburban in character...even though they are in fact firmly part of automobile-era suburbs. Garreau's book was in part a hymn to the energy and imagination of large-scale real estate developers, and novelist Tom Wolfe has his flamboyant character Charlie Croker in *A Man in Full* (1998) muse on the way that the book put a name to the type of real estate deals that he had been pursuing instinctively.

Edge cities are New Towns without the tracts of housing, making it attractive to North American urban planners and public officials wanting to bring order out of the randomness of the commercial real estate market but not wanting to venture into New Town territory. Several cities in the later 1980s or 1990s adopted plans that promoted the development of outlying centers or nodes as junior edge cities. Phoenix talked about promoting "urban villages." The Puget Sound Regional Council defined nine established downtowns in the Seattle–Tacoma area and twelve suburban locations as "urban centers" that are to absorb most new employment and receive most transportation improvements. Vancouver's regional growth strategy identifies eight regional centers outside the city itself.

Edge city is an American coinage, but other nations have their own toned-down versions where retail complexes and office buildings offer corporations proximity to each other and alternatives to central cites. The Santa Fe development outside Mexico City was built with the explicit goal of housing multinational corporations. Espoo grew from a sleepy fringe of Helsinki to Finland's tech center with companies like Nokia. Croydon on the south side of London has sprouted glass towers. The southern fringe of Berlin has accreted research and development facilities and tech manufacturing since German reunification. Flughafen Zurich draws corporate offices to the city's north side and Amsterdam's Schiphol Airport has attracted offices just as Chicago's O'Hare has done. The Marne-la-Vallée district east of Paris has brought French New Town planning, the new Université Gustav Eiffel, and Disneyland Paris together in a new suburban landscape.

Knowledge suburbs

The hottest sector of the twenty-first-century economy is overwhelmingly suburban. Silicon Valley is a trope and a reality, an economic cluster and a particular suburban environment that is envied and partially reproduced in Austin, Texas; London's M4 Corridor; Bangalore; and Guadalajara. It was the prototype for a suburban region with an economy built around the development and exploitation of information.

Palo Alto is the epicenter. Faculty from Stanford University, led by provost Frederick Terman, developed Stanford Research Park as a business park where academic ideas could be turned into marketable innovations. Early successes like Hewlett-Packard were a magnet for researchers, corporate start-ups, and, perhaps most important, federal government contracts and venture capital. The 1950s and 1960s were the hardware era when defense contracts ruled, Lockheed Missiles and Space Company was the largest employer, and engineers were straight-laced Republicans with their sleeves rolled up. The consumer-oriented tech business incubated in the 1970s and took off in the 1980s with personal computing. The name Silicon Valley dates to the 1980s when engineers found their work enlivened by brasher entrepreneurs with marketing savvy. That was also the decade when Boston lost the public relations battle. Despite its huge reservoir of technical expertise, its tech companies were just too boring compared to the frat house excess and exuberance of California. In turn, the hardware era set the stage for a new Silicon Valley era that depended on the expansion of the internet and has come like a tidal wave of I-thises, I-thats, and apps, where real money is to be made by platforms like Google and Facebook that deal in providing information as a service rather than selling information hardware. The old Santa Clara valley was farmland. The new Silicon Valley was a "futuretown" with plenty of low-slung buildings with green or blue tinted glass behind swatches of grass. Some massive additions include the Googleplex and Apple's circular headquarters, which resembles either a particle accelerator or a slice of pineapple.

The Silicon Valley model has shaped global suburbs. Dozens have aspired to be the "silicon next," whether or not they hope to produce silicon-based processing chips. Sometimes they succeed. A semicircle of high-tech companies rings the north side of Austin. The French government located several research institutes and universities in Massy–Saclay southwest of Paris, an attractive area with nice parks and middle-class housing; private research and development companies followed. The district is sometimes branded as Saclay–Scientipôle or Cité Scientifique Sud de Paris. Indian prime minister Jawaharlal Nehru in 1961 called Bangalore India's City of the Future. There was steady growth of peripheral research campuses in the twentieth century; zooming growth in the twenty-first century has consolidated a wide high-tech arc on the city's east side. Queenstown, originally a satellite residential area on the western outskirts of central Singapore, took off in the twenty-first century as home to an imposing group of universities, tech corporations, and research centers with names like Biopolis and Fusionopolis.

The futuretown look is an international fashion statement. Globetrotting architects and consultants from San Francisco and Singapore take the same design models to one aspiring country after another. Global circulation of real estate and planning expertise shapes compatible business and residential spaces— landscaped low-rise research parks for workers, gated American-style estates for their families. The intention is to create a comfortable environment that executives and engineers from Germany, Australia, Canada, Israel, and the United States can all find compatible. It is a suburban equivalent of increasingly identical "global city" centers that provide standard housing and amenities whether one is in London or Los Angeles, Sydney or San Francisco.

Knowledge suburbs go silicon suburbs one better. The latter tend to create hardware and software for trading on information more than they create new knowledge, traditionally the province of universities ensconced in cities like Chicago, Melbourne, Munich, and Paris and older suburbs like Cambridge, Massachusetts, and

Berkeley, California. The Japanese government tried to change the game with Tsukuba Science City, thirty-five miles from Tokyo, designed as a very particular type of New Town. It was the site for the 1986 International Science Technology Exposition. Half of Japan's public research budget goes to its two universities and dozens of public research institutes, which seed private companies in the Silicon Valley mode. Kansei Science City between Kyoto, Osaka, and Nara is another national project on the same model with universities, research industries, and tech centers in several research campuses.

China's knowledge suburbs include entire new satellite cities anchored by university campuses. Students and staff fill new housing and patronize shopping; Guangzhou University Town has ten institutions and tens of thousands of students. In the United States new universities may be contributors to general-issue suburban growth, like the University of Texas, Arlington, or one part of a planned new town, like the University of California, Irvine. In Japan and China, universities and research complexes are the reason that knowledge suburbs exist.

Chapter 6
What's wrong with suburbs

In the great comic film *Mon Oncle* (1959), actor-director Jacques Tati plays Monsieur Hulot, a bemused and befuddled observer of modern life. Hulot lives in a picturesque old city neighborhood in a rickety walk-up apartment. Everyone knows everyone else and charming "Paris music" plays in the background. When he visits his sister and her factory-executive husband, the music stops, and the scene shifts to a severely modern house where the garage holds a big new American automobile and where nobody has any fun (except for the audience). The past contrasts with the present, tradition with modernity, and working-class camaraderie with suburban pretension.

Mon Oncle is a gentle addition to a well-established tradition of suburb bashing. Suburbs have had defenders, but the predominant commentary has emphasized their problems and flaws. Journalists and intellectuals have tended to see themselves as sophisticated and cosmopolitan city people for whom suburbs are unfamiliar ground, a sort of social void between vibrant city streets and peaceful countryside. Back in 1876, an anonymous British writer in the *Architect* complained that "a modern suburb is neither one thing nor the other. It has neither the advantages of the town nor the open freedom of the country, but manages to combine in nice equality of proportion the disadvantages of both."

10. Postwar suburbia was an object of satire on both sides of the Atlantic. The French film *Mon Oncle* (1958) poked fun at the sterility of new Parisian suburbs through the figure of M. Hulot, who lives in a traditional neighborhood, dresses most unfashionably in hat and raincoat, and visits his sister's new house as if he is visiting another planet.

Boringly bourgeois

Complaints about suburbs surfaced in Britain when the mortar was scarcely dry between the bricks in new terraces and semidetached houses. The problem was no longer that suburbs were dens of danger harboring thieves and cutpurses. Rather, as bland breeders of middle-class conformity and complacency, suburbs now were not dangerous enough. The prolific novelist George Gissing, who preferred more stylish parts of London, reluctantly lived for several years in Camberwell. *In the Year of Jubilee* (1894) was his revenge, calling out the new suburb as the epitome of mass society shallowness that his heroine was desperate to escape. C. F. G. Masterman was a left-leaning journalist who confidently published *The Condition of England* in 1909. He was not pleased with the new suburbs, where working-class families were finding their first decent housing and the middle class was finding some elbow room, because he found them too bland, quiet, and comfortable to generate any social change. Indeed, such new districts populated by "suburbans" were the target of critics from both the left and the right as places both bland and boring. Journalists blasted the monotony of the new cityscape, and the novelists took aim at the bourgeois trap of suburban life. Bestselling novelist and popular historian Walter Besant bemoaned "the life of the suburb without any society; no social gatherings or institutions; as dull a life as mankind ever tolerated."

George Orwell formed an antipathy to the vacuous villa neighborhoods of Britain's imperial administrators during several years in government service in Burma in the 1920s. *A Clergyman's Daughter* (1935) describes "a repellent suburb ten or a dozen miles from London...labyrinths of meanly decent streets, all so indistinguishably alike." *Coming Up for Air* (1939) encompasses many facets of the indictment. George Bowling, a forty-five-year-old insurance salesman living in an inner-outer suburb of London, treats his mid-life crisis by trying and failing to revisit his nostalgically remembered childhood. The book opens with a long soliloquy in which Bowling excoriates his neighborhood. Long, identical rows of semidetached houses "fester." Husbands who will never be taken for gentlemen all catch the 8:21 into the city. "What is a road like Ellesmere Road?" he asks. "Just a prison with the cells all in a row. A line of semidetached torture-chambers where the poor little five-to-ten-pound-a-weekers quake and shiver, every one of them with the boss twisting his tail and his wife riding him." The place and the people—all the boring sameness.

The critique easily crossed oceans. George Babbitt, the hero in Sinclair Lewis's 1922 novel *Babbitt*, set in a fast-growing city something like Cincinnati or Indianapolis, is more financially secure than George Bowling. He likes his new house and neighborhood, but he too tries unsuccessfully to break the bonds of bourgeois boredom, living it up on a convention junket to the big city but deciding that there's no place like home. Like Orwell, Lewis pondered the way that suburban life killed the dreams of middle-class men. Neither seemed as concerned about the wives.

Pleasant suburban comedies of manners could scarcely hold their own against such literary firepower, but they did put women at the center. In William Pett Ridge's *A Clever Wife* (1896), a move to Clapham Common allows the title character to support her husband's career and save their marriage. In *The Smiths of Surbiton* (1906), a rising clerk and his new wife use family money to happily lease a five-bedroom house in "a smart place like Surbiton." The novel is a series of vignettes about adjusting to middle-class suburbia where "it is just as easy to make acquaintances...as it is difficult to make friends." A generation later, the much weightier if eccentric writer Stevie Smith praised her outer London suburb of Palmers Green for its friendliness, fresh air, children, and roses, exemplars of the blandness that many others disliked. She inventoried the names of its pubs and the names that homeowners write on their garden gates, the clubs and entertainments, the cheerful Christianity, the park where on "a fine Sunday afternoon you may snuff the quick-witted, high-lying life of a true suburban community," and "the family life behind the fishnet curtains—father's chair, uproar, dogs, babies and radio."

Smith would have found some agreement across the Atlantic. Everyday Americans in the 1920s applauded the suburban trend, which was making attractive, low-density neighborhoods available to millions of affluent and ordinary citizens. Government officials praised the normalcy of suburban life. Planners and reformers had battled the congestion of the industrial city for decades. They now looked to carefully controlled suburban growth as a sovereign remedy for urban ills. The alternative to "Dinosaur Cities," said the urban planner Clarence Stein, was "a beautiful environment, a home for children, an opportunity to enjoy the day's leisure" in a new community. Echoing Adna Weber from a quarter century earlier, sociologist Harlan Paul Douglass examined *The Suburban Trend* in 1925 and concluded that "a crowded world must be either suburban or savage."

Disappointment and disdain

When Lewis Mumford published *The City in History* in 1961, three decades of public advocacy, thick books on cities and technology, and contributions as the architecture critic for *The New Yorker* had made him America's best-known commentator on cities. In the 1930s, he had been a leading champion of urban regionalism and decentralization on the Garden City model. The new book was magisterial and sometimes misguided, and it had a different message. Americans after World War II may have followed his advice to move outward from the city, but they had gone about it wrong. A single paragraph about recent suburbs contained the modifiers "common," "unidentifiable," "inflexibly," "uniform" (four times), and "same" (five times), recycling George Orwell's scorn for "indistinguishably alike" semidetached houses for the new postwar Levittown era. Mumford's longtime associate Catherine Bauer edited a special issue of *Architectural Forum* that asserted, "The last ten years have given us am unholy mess of land use, land coverage, congestion and ugliness.... [W]e have no way to avert this crisis of growth, no choice but to face it and try to civilize it."

Critics in the 1950s and 1960s added new themes to the prewar critique. Lewis Mumford was bitterly disappointed that his vision of infinite garden suburbs had yielded mass-produced suburbs instead. Left-wing critics decried suburbs for destroying working-class militance, one of the reasons why the singer-songwriter Malvina Reynolds wrote "Little Boxes," with its disdain for ticky-tacky houses. The aesthetic attack on "sprawl" and sameness continued, but with added social dimensions. They were still bad for men, but now also for women and perhaps even children, despite the apparently happy kids in *Leave It to Beaver* or *E.T.* British experts blamed their country's New Towns for the erosion of community ties.

Americans have many noncomplimentary words for peripheral neighborhoods. There is the dismissive *'burbs*. There are *slurb* and *sloburb* and *sprawl* as expletives. In the decades following World War II, journalists and pop sociologists accused suburbs of being transient, conservative, materialistic, conformist, and superficial. They found social disorganization and narrow individualism, when individualism was not being overwhelmed by frantic neighboring. Suburban children were being coddled into wimps with no ambition. Or perhaps they were being set on the path that would make them other-directed corporate drones. Or perhaps permissive upbringing allowed them to run wild, stealing hubcaps, disrespecting their elders, and terrorizing the streets with drag races—see *Rebel without a Cause* (1955).

The authors of *The Split-Level Trap* (1960) cherry-picked interviews with New Jerseyites to paint a disturbing picture of "disturbia" filled with stressed and dangerous men, uncontrolled children, and confused and lonely women. Observers noted the new suburbs had plenty of churches and church-going families, which should presumably be encouraging. No, said Gibson Winter in *The Suburban Captivity of the Churches* (1961), shallow suburban religion sapped the resources of inner-city churches and was a pallid substitute for the real thing. The critique has enjoyed a vigorous afterlife, particularly in James Howard Kunstler's thin but popular polemic *The Geography of Nowhere: The Rise and Decline of America's Man-Made Landscape* (1994).

American commentators, who tended to be liberal Democrats, also found it hard to accept that voters really preferred Dwight

Eisenhower to Adlai Stevenson in the 1952 and 1956 presidential elections and feared that suburban materialism was turning voters from Democrats to Republicans. Their diagnosis was wrong. If there was a change agent, it was national prosperity and an expanding middle class, not an accident of residence. When auto workers moved from Oakland to Milpitas, California, for jobs in a suburban Ford plant that opened in 1955, their affiliations did not change. They preferred their new homes because of better quality and more respectable addresses, but they showed no inclination to cut off ties to the city they had left behind or to change their political values.

Residents of Levittown, New Jersey, about fifteen miles from Philadelphia, felt much the same way. Herbert Gans, a professor of city planning and sociology at the University of Pennsylvania, surprised his urban colleagues by packing up his family and belongings and joining the first wave of new Levittowners in 1958. He found that 85 percent of his new neighbors preferred the suburbs for the down-to-earth reason that they offered the best and biggest house for the money. Good schools and convenient shopping ranked almost as high. Few Levittowners were changed by their new environment. Fewer still thought that there was any reason to feel embarrassed about a home in suburbia. For many of them, after all, the realistic alternative to Levittown was a crowded walk-up apartment or a South Philly row house shared with the in-laws.

The English researchers Michael Young and Peter Willmott addressed the same question by studying working-class families who moved from London's Bethnal Green to a new suburban housing estate. Interviews and surveys for *Family and Kinship in East London* (1957) led them to conclude that social networks fragmented and that depression and anxiety increased. Women in particular missed socializing on crowded streets and having daily chats with their mums. The results were popularized as the social problem of "New Town blues."

The popular version went well beyond the data. Studies of Harlow, Crawley, and Graydon made clear that *suburb* was not the variable that predicted stress and dissatisfaction. The transition from one place to another was difficult, not the new suburb in itself, which had many advantages of more modern housing. Residents of Worsley, a new neighborhood on the outskirts of Manchester, had moved from Salford, the iconic "dirty old town" of Ewan MacColl's song. The critique would suggest that they would have missed the old town. Instead, they overwhelmingly preferred the new.

Betty Friedan identified an American version of New Town malaise in her powerful bestseller *The Feminine Mystique* (1963). The mystique was a set of social values that isolated women within nuclear households, enforced domesticity, and blocked access to fulfilling careers. It was a societal problem, but it was easy to identify with suburbs. Friedan, a labor journalist and political activist who somewhat misleadingly presented herself as another suburban housewife, likened suburbs to comfortable concentration camps. A decade later, Ira Levin carried the metaphor of disempowerment to a logic extreme in *The Stepford Wives* (1972, film version 1975), which imagines suburban Connecticut housewives replaced by androids.

The suburbs that Friedan considered traps that disempowered women ironically opened doors to political influence. Suburbs were indeed communities filled with newcomers who often lacked ties and obligations to extended families, churches, and other community institutions. Women who had satisfied their responsibilities to their nuclear families were relatively free to give time and energy to political activity. At the same time, spreading suburbs were "frontiers" that called for concerted action to solve immediate needs such as adequate schools and decent parks. Since pursuit of such services has often been viewed as women's work, in contrast to the men's work of economic development, burgeoning suburbs offered numerous chances to engage in civic work, to sharpen skills as political activists, and finally to run for local office. Their campaigns were aided by the fact that suburbs lacked the entrenched political machines of older cities with open races for school boards, city councils, and state legislative seats. They ranged the political spectrum from progressive League of Women Voters members to deeply conservative women fighting communist infiltration of public schools, but all took advantage of suburban opportunities.

Popular culture has its own mixed take on the myth of suburban malaise. Paul McCartney remembered the "blue suburban skies" of Mossley Hill on the south side of Liverpool. He and John Lennon changed buses at the shelter on the roundabout on Penny Lane as they traveled between each other's houses. Other rock bands would have none of this nostalgia. The Sex Pistols' "Satellite" (1977) characteristically addresses a string of insults to suburban kids unfortunate enough to live outside London. The Canadian rockers Rush released "Subdivisions" in 1982; the lyrics cycle through variations on one-sided and insulated suburban conformity that drives dreamers and misfits to the city.

On both sides of the Atlantic, 1970s and 1980s television updated the earlier comedy of manners with sitcoms that offered a relatively benign view of suburban life. Television writers and executives viewed cities as the proper setting for crime and detective series and for comedies about young single people. But the suburbs were the place for family comedies. Britain's *Bless This House* (1971–76) was set in Putney, *Happy Ever After* (1974–79) in Ealing, and *The Good Life* (1975–78) in Surbiton—all of them London suburbs. *The Brady Bunch* (1969–74) brought American sitcomland to Los Angeles, *Family Ties* (1982–89) to suburban Columbus, Ohio, *Home Improvement* (1991–99) to suburban Detroit, *Third Rock from the Sun* (1996–2001) to suburban Cleveland, and *Everybody Loves Raymond* (1996–2005) to Lynbrook, Long Island. Only in the twenty-first century would crime come to the suburbs in a big way with *The Sopranos* (1999–2007), *Breaking Bad* (2008–13), and Britain's much fluffier

Murder in Suburbia (2004–5). The generalization remains: for television, suburbs are usually nicer places than cities.

Paving paradise

When Joni Mitchell sang about paving paradise for a parking lot in "Big Yellow Taxi" (1970), listeners joined an ongoing conversation and encapsulated a suburban dilemma. The contrast between Honolulu's concrete cityscape and its green mountain backdrop was the inspiration for the line, but it resonated with people who had moved to be closer to rural landscapes only to find even newer subdivisions and housing estates consuming that very countryside. Images of bulldozers uprooting California citrus trees and plowing under Long Island potato fields for new subdivisions were part of the broad indictment of sprawl. Australians fretted as Melbourne suburbs consumed pastoral orchards and market gardens. New suburbanites quickly realized that more development—the tract houses built after their own—eroded the access to rural amenities that were a supposed suburban attraction. The animated film *Pom Poko* was number one at the Japanese box office in 1994. Its storyline follows the efforts of *tanuki*, or Japanese raccoon dogs, to protect their native forest from massive development that is transforming the Tama Hills outside Tokyo into housing for 200,000 people.

Leapfrog development not only consumed the very landscapes that attracted people out of cities in the first place, but also brought additional problems. Overburdened roads, never designed for heavy use, created traffic jams and air pollution. Builders often installed septic tanks rather than more expensive sewer systems; as the population grew and overburdened the soil, contamination bubbled to the surface and seeped into streams. Rachel Carson's bestselling *Silent Spring* (1962) documented far-reaching impacts of pesticides, but its most vivid imagery was the imagined disappearance of songbirds from suburban backyards. Journalist William H. Whyte played a leading role in

11. Traffic jams and tie-ups are an inescapable feature of automobile-based suburbanization, as in this image of a tailback on the M-25 motorway that encircles London. Freeway gridlock is a strong argument for more effective planning of compact cities with good public transportation. It has also become a cinematic staple, igniting vigilante rage in *Falling Down* but triggering spontaneous dancing across stalled cars in *La La Land*.

identifying the suburban environmental crisis. In magazines like *Life* and *Fortune* he made an impassioned case for preserving open space as metropolitan areas grew:

> Here, in which was pleasant countryside only a year ago, is the sight of what is to come. No more sweep of green—across the hills are spattered scores of random subdivisions, each laid out in the same dreary asphalt curves. Gone are the streams, brooks, woods and forests, that the subdivisions' signs talked about. The streams are largely buried in concrete culverts. Where one flows briefly through a patch of weeds and tin cans it is fetid with the ooze of septic tanks.

Environmentalism was certainly about preserving the magnificent forests, canyons, and wilderness, but it was also about keeping suburbia from fouling its own nest. The conservation generals who had first focused on protecting western wilderness found that suburbanites with local concerns were foot soldiers who could effectively pressure state legislatures and Congress. They wanted to save the Grand Canyon for their summer vacations, but they also wanted to keep the patch of woods across the street and the farms down the road—so long as the farmers did not rev up their tractors too early in the morning. Congress responded with a wave of environmental laws in the early 1970s, establishing the Environmental Protection Agency and passing the Clean Air Act and Clean Water Act. Local governments responded by approving clustered development plans, establishing suburb park districts, and investing in sewer systems.

Farmland protection and greenbelts were tools that protected open space while enhancing the value of adjacent land, a win–win for more affluent suburbanites. Oregon preserved farmland by requiring urban growth boundaries to slow the outward expansion of its cities. British Columbia designated agricultural reserves around Vancouver. Melbourne is ringed by a dozen "green wedges" outside an urban growth boundary. The Netherlands designated a "green heart" encircled by Amsterdam, The Hague, and

Rotterdam. Greenbelts around major cities limit development on 13 percent of the land in England.

The environmental critique of suburbanization and responses in the twentieth century were shared internationally, but the issues were essentially local: what was happening around Vancouver or Manchester or Tokyo and what to do about it. In the twenty-first century the critique went global along with rising concern about climate change. Low-density suburbs with little mixing of different land uses and poorly connected streets promote individual automobile use and transportation choices that consume more energy per person than denser development. Studies comparing Australian and American cities and US city subareas show that low-density land development adds to the atmospheric carbon burden. The remedies are better public transportation options and mixed-use development that reduces the need for multiple long journeys.

Inefficient localism

Citizens and bureaucrats seldom see eye to eye about regional planning. Suburbanites place a high value on political localism in which relatively small municipalities can pursue their own development plans and fend off unwanted initiatives. This is true in France, Hungary, and China as well as in the United States, and it deeply frustrates officials who must plan and implement infrastructure for entire metropolitan regions. The tension between local choice and regional efficiency and equity plays out in both theoretical debates and efforts to devise schemes for metropolitan governance, which have taken hundreds of different forms and are subject to changing agendas of provincial and national governments.

Americans are especially prone to metropolitan fragmentation. Ring after ring of smaller municipalities engird Chicago and St. Louis. Add special-function agencies like water districts and transit agencies to the mix and the result can be confusing to citizens and frustrating to officials. The New York region, according to a classic analysis, had more than 1,400 governments in 1960 trying to manage a single functioning metropolis. The United States is not alone. London's thirty-two boroughs are part of Greater London, but they are jealous of their prerogatives. Melbourne's five million people are parceled among twenty-seven cities and four more rural shires. The enthusiastically local French divvy the two million people of metropolitan Lyon among more than 500 small municipalities.

One problem is technocratic. Highways, public transit, water supply, and sewers are area-wide systems that require regional planning and management. However, authority is often fragmented along localities and divided among different functions, meaning that highway planning and transit planning may be handled by completely different organizations. Responsibilities can be divided even within a single category. In Portland, Oregon, the state manages several through highways, the city deals with surface streets, the county maintains bridges across the Willamette River, and other agencies manage transit and the airport. The results can be public confusion and waste of public funds. Moreover, individual municipalities may be able to veto valuable regional investments. Depending on one's point of view, divided power stymies progress or blocks overreaching bureaucracies from trampling local interests.

A second problem is economic. Suburban governments compete with each other and with the central city for new investment that may provide local jobs or increase local taxes. Local governments in the United States depend heavily on property taxes, which gives them an incentive to attract commercial and industrial uses that have high value and low service costs while fending off affordable apartments. In effect, each suburb wants the shopping mall but wants the customers to live in the next town over, which will have to pay for schools and parks. A suburb may be tempted to offer financial inducements to a "clean" industry, for example. The move makes local political sense, but it is macroeconomic idiocy. When every locality is trying the same tactic, the public sector loses in the aggregate and the total economy is less efficient. In China, land beyond municipal boundaries is collectively owned by rural townships. In theory, their role is to preserve rural uses. In recent fact, townships have been developing their own apartment projects to generate revenue. They sell apartments with murky legal title for less than the cost of sanctioned apartments, meeting a real housing need but inefficiently competing with each other.

The third problem with fragmented government is inequity. Control of land uses allows localities to use exclusionary policies to exclude poor people and, by implication, members of racial and ethnic groups with relatively low wealth and income. This has worked in tandem with private real estate discrimination against members of religious groups such as Jews. This is not just an American problem. The affluent peripheral municipalities on the west side of Lyon have successfully fought off increased densities, retaining their semirural character, while the working-class east side has absorbed high-rise housing and immigration. A market-based political science theory known as public choice suggests that metropolitan fragmentation is a good thing because it allows people to choose their service package. One municipality puts more funding into parks and another into libraries, and you can choose which you prefer. That is fine if "you" are white and middle class and can actually make choices. Poor people with limited resources, and limited by systemic racism, can find that choice is an empty promise, and the core of the theory crashes.

New and often well-funded schools have been one of the great attractions of American suburbs. They also demonstrate the problems of government fragmentation. In the United States, local districts that set their own policies run most state-funded or common schools. There are more than 10,000 such school districts, some with a couple hundred students and others with tens of thousands. Nobody will ever doubt the maxim "all politics is local" after they have attended a school board meeting that deals with changes to curriculum or sports programs. Schools can also be prizes in racial conflicts, because some suburbanites take the "whiteness" of a suburban school as an indicator of its superiority.

In two key cases, the US Supreme Court set a hard boundary between city and suburban school districts. *Swann v. Charlotte-Mecklenburg Board of Education* (1971) held that crosstown busing of students is an acceptable way to racially integrate public schools that would otherwise be segregated because of neighborhood residential segregation. In *Milliken v. Bradley* (1974), however, it also held that the remedy of busing was confined to individual school districts, effectively insulating predominatly white suburbs with independent districts. The desire to avoid integrated schools causes suburbs to fiercely defend their political independence. In Denver, for example, by-products of a bitter debate over court-enforced busing included the incorporation or expansion of several large suburbs and a state constitutional amendment that made it impossible for the city of Denver, and thus the Denver school district, to expand its boundaries.

Technocrats and policy wonks often suggest that the solution is to create a metro-wide government. This solution can work for single functions such as transportation or air-quality regulation, but comprehensive metropolitan governments are rare. Local resistance can be strong. Suburbanites did not want to share the problems and costs of poorer cities. Residents and political leaders in old cities do not want their influence diluted by adding more middle-class or racial majority voters. They do not want to see local planning authority diluted, as when the city of Paris opposed the powers given the Métropole du Grand Paris that the national government created in 2016. Moreover, centralized governments that create institutions of metropolitan governance can also take them away. Harold Wilson's Labour government created the

Greater London Council in 1965, Margaret Thatcher's Conservative government abolished it in 1986, and Tony Blair's Labour government created the Greater London Authority in 2000.

Suburban inefficiency is a technocratic critique that excites political scientists and planners more than regular citizens, and solutions are always subject to politics. Every nation, and sometimes every province and state, has its own laws and rules within which metropolitan coordination functions, or fails to. There are plenty of promising efforts, but no common solution that fits all places and nations. Rock stars do not write songs about regional tax base sharing, nor do novelists pivot plots on the fate of Metro Toronto, although to everyone's enlightenment the television comedy *Parks and Recreation* did take up the political and social challenges of merging down-to-earth Pawnee, Indiana, with snobby adjacent Eagleton.

Crabgrass chaos: failed suburbs in science fiction

Suburbs have not fared well in North American speculative fiction. Hollywood disaster movies may prefer spectacular scenes of imploding downtowns, but three generations of science fiction writers have seen the suburbs as the place where society will unravel and turn savage. They have offered variations on the theme of crabgrass chaos, projecting aging suburbs as the new ghettos and slums, zones of danger and depopulation where it is everyone for themselves and wilding gangs take the weak.

Take the modest suburban house in the fictional suburb of Belle Reve, New Jersey, whose picture window is marred by a long crack from top to bottom. The house features in Frederick Pohl and Cyril Kornbluth's 1955 novel *Gladiator-at-Law*, set in a socially divided twenty-first-century America. With the severe housing shortage of the late 1940s a recent memory, Pohl and Kornbluth open with World War II veterans lining up to view Belle Reve's model homes—a scene that mirrored real communities like Lakewood and Levittown. In the novel, things turn sour fast. The tiny houses are only partly finished. Unexpected fees and taxes for schools, fire protection, and sewers eat up money that might have gone to fix the window. The market for the houses dries up as newer neighborhoods are built, and bad elements move in, including moonshiners with a still in their living room [it would now be a meth house].

By 2040 the once hopeful community has turned into the nasty and brutish slum of Belly Rave. Some of the houses are burned out shells; others have turned into dens of vice. The house in which the Bligh family lives may be the same that we saw generations earlier. The roof leaks, the stairs are rotten, and the cracked window is now boarded over, with just a chink left for scoping out dangers in the front yard. People huddle in their houses with guns at the ready. Thrill-seekers arrive for illicit sex, but the city police come only in armored cars. Reflecting the postwar era's overblown panic about juvenile delinquency, Pohl and Kornbluth envisioned gangs of preteens and teens roaming the streets, protecting themselves to avoid being sold as pickpockets and child prostitutes.

In 1956, journalist John Keats titled his antisuburb diatribe *The Crack in the Picture Window*. A signature feature of atomic age residential design, the cracked window was a multiple metaphor, calling out the suburbs for failing as physical places and for betraying expectations as harmonious communities. Pohl and Kornbluth extrapolated this disdain with which intellectuals in the 1950s treated the massive growth of middle-class suburbs, producing an early example of a recurring science fiction vision of feral suburbia.

A generation after *Gladiator-at-Law*, suburban California attracted the same sort of science fiction critique. The antisuburban indictment had moved beyond the moral and aesthetic posture of the 1950s to an explicitly political argument about the economic polarization of the metroscape. Coming soon to Southern California, or already arrived, said novelists and social scientists alike, is a metropolis deeply divided by economic class and race.

The decrepit Los Angeles in Cynthia Kadohata's *In the Heart of the Valley of Love* (1992) is facing a death spiral. Francie is nineteen years old in 2052. With her parents dead of a wasting disease that is a metaphor for cultural malaise and economic decline, she is living in a run-down bungalow and working for a financially marginal delivery service. A new highway system looms unfinished, started "before everything ran out of money, back at the beginning of the century." The family house, bought by her great-great-grandmother, is now "in a section of town largely abandoned by anyone who mattered to the country's economy." Francie sometimes wakes to the smell of burning buildings not many blocks away. Meanwhile, the people of "richtown" (her term for places like Brentwood) are increasingly moving to "camps," communities "enclosed by high metal fences and guarded by uniformed, armed men and women." We can assume that Kadohata picked the term *camp* to recall the Japanese American incarceration experience of 1942–45 and relishes the inversion of the image as the elite pull barbed wire around themselves rather than stringing it around others.

Octavia Butler's *Parable of the Sower* (1993) is perhaps the most wrenchingly realized of gated suburb fictions. Fortress LA is now literal, and the extinction of the middle plays out in fire and blood. The novel centers on Lauren Olamina, who grows up in the 2020s in a collapsing Los Angeles. Her parents and the other homeowners have created the ultimate cul-de-sac, surrounding their street of eleven houses with a locked gate and wall that is "three meters high and topped off with pieces of broken glass as well as the usual barbed wire." The internal combustion era is over, with three-car garages turned into rabbit hutches and chicken coops. Lauren's walled street is in the San Fernando valley, a sad survivor of the valley isolationism described by Mike Davis. Adults venture out for jobs or errands, but never at night and seldom alone. The whole community learns to handle guns; the only safe respite from the tiny community is a group excursion for target practice in the surrounding ravines where they are likely to encounter homeless squatters, wild dogs, and human corpses.

As the story unfolds, addicts and thieves grow bolder, scaling the wall and cutting the razor wire, first to strip the gardens, then to ransack houses for anything they can sell. Three years after the story opens—it is now 2027 and Lauren is eighteen—the community dies in a night of riot and fire, murder and rape. She escapes by luck, returns in the morning to ash-covered bodies, salvages what she can, and starts a long trek north on what will be the road to a new, hard-won, tentative, and very rural utopia.

Americans have continued to vote with their Chevys and Buicks, making the nation officially suburban in 2000, but the suburban triumph can also be read as a suburban crisis. As early as the 1980s, social scientists realized that the aging of the baby boom generation meant that demand for housing was stagnant and declining numbers of students were rattling around in schools built for Brady Bunch families. The housing crash of 2008 fueled a wave of commentary about the rise of "slumburbia." Older suburbs in the Rust Belt and new suburbs in the Sun Belt were both described as losing the middle class, falling into abandonment and disrepair, attracting vandals, becoming homes to drug gangs. The urban crisis rhetoric of the 1960s and 1970s was thus transferred part and parcel to the suburbs of the new century.

Novelist Douglas Coupland has a particular fascination with abandoned suburbs—portraying a "bleached and defoliated Flintstones color cartoon of a failed housing development" in *Generation X* (1991), an abandoned and burned-out shopping mall in *Shampoo Planet* (1992), and an empty corporate research campus with an *Andromeda Strain* ambiance in *Microserfs* (1995). He takes ruin to an uncanny extreme in *Girlfriend in a Coma* (1998). Two-thirds of the way through a satirical comedy of manners, everyone in the world falls into a deep coma except for a handful of friends who watch the collapse of Vancouver from their North Shore suburb, leaving them to wander the cul-de-sacs looking for prescription drugs and raiding the Park Royal Mall for booze. The end of the world arrives not with aliens zapping the Eiffel Tower but with the supposed social vacuity of suburbia taken to the extreme of eerie emptiness of the sort that social critics have long feared.

Battleground L.A.

Los Angeles looms large in American responses to modern suburbs, a landscape on which to project fears and expectations as the "ultimate city." Los Angeles has long been easy to caricature as "nineteen suburbs in search of a metropolis," in a 1925 comment by Aldous Huxley, or "seventy-two suburbs in search of a city," an acerbic line that Dorothy Parker never actually penned. Journalist Richard Elman traveled to the inner suburb of Compton "with the thought in mind that this was the future ... what lies in store for all the new suburbs of all the big cities of America." Mike Davis castigated the isolationism of the "suburban badlands" in *City of Quartz* (1990). To the contrary, Los Angeles suburbia evoked freedom for British architecture critic Reyner Banham in *The Architecture of the Four Ecologies* (1971) and for British painter David Hockney in a series of sun-drenched canvases.

Los Angeles roads and freeways loom large in judgments about American suburbia. The character Lauren Olamina escapes the dying city by trekking along the 118 expressway. Joan Didion sends Maria Wyeth driving the freeways for endless, aimless nights in her novel *Play It as It Lays* (1970) in a metaphor of alienation, but Pasadena's wide Colorado Boulevard means freedom to Mildred Pierce as green lights pace her speeding car (it is a street that Pasadena native Octavia Butler knew well). Consider two cinematic traffic jams. One pushes an unemployed aerospace engineer over the edge in *Falling Down* (1993). He abandons his car and embarks on an increasingly violent traverse from Pasadena to the sea. Filming was aptly interrupted by the disorder that followed the acquittal of Rodney King's assailants. More than three decades later and in a happier city, motorists respond to a traffic jam on an elevated freeway by exiting their cars for a spontaneous dance number in *La La Land* (2016).

D. J. Waldie lives in the Lakewood ranch house that his father bought in the first years after World War II. *Holy Land: A Suburban Memoir* (1996, 2005) mixes fragments of history, observation, and autobiography to excavate the sense of place that even a nondescript suburb can nurture. This is not an exercise in personal nostalgia. Instead, Lakewood stands in for whole suburban generations who have lived in tract houses in neighborhoods of other tract houses. Waldie sees life behind the anonymity, creativity within the grid. French sociologist Michel de Certeau argued the difference between the abstract city seen from a skyscraper and the lived experience of city people observed on the streets. Waldie makes the same point about a series of aerial photographs of Lakewood under construction. Appearing in dozens of books about architecture and planning, the images turn the suburb into a metaphor of industrial uniformity. Waldie will have none of it, reminding readers that the houses would be occupied by real people who would learn to play hide-and-seek and build full suburban lives in the backyards, parks, streets, and schools.

Chapter 7

Two hundred years
and counting

Suburbs are continually evolving, even if the feral future that is
popular in science fiction is unlikely. Suburban development is
neither a villain nor a hero for the twenty-first century. Hundreds
of millions of people will continue to live in old and new suburbs,
and their challenge will be to devise and support ways in which
their residential choices can help to maintain a livable planet in
the face of unprecedented stress from climate change and
transitions in energy regimes.

Suburbanization in the coming decades will be marked by
the continued interchange of ideas about how to shape
environmentally and financially sustainable communities.
This sort of interchange has long been characteristic of urban
development. It intensified in the industrial era as city builders in
the Americas eagerly copied Europe, and European colonialists
imposed their styles of urban planning on Asia and Africa. Both
the United States and the Soviet Union after World War II made
the export of their specific models of suburbanization an element
of their foreign policies.

Twenty-first-century information networks are just as complex
and intense. Models for suburban development continue to flow
outward from the North Atlantic world via private consultants,
visiting academic experts, investors, and international real estate

firms. They also flow among Asian, African, and Latin American nations through the same sorts of channels while informing American and European practice through international organizations and consultations.

California dreaming

Wooded hills that rise on the southern margins of Sofia, Bulgaria, display the international attraction of affluent American suburbia. In the socialist era, bureaucrats and professionals added weekend dachas to the scattered villages, with limited impact on the rural landscape. In the 1990s, however, weekendland morphed into Sofia's new suburban zone. Old socialists retired and turned their retreats into permanent houses, while families with new money seized on the advantages of leafy living. They peppered the landscape with large new houses and walled compounds, scorning the "old socs" who were their neighbors. Developers liked the appeal of American-sounding names like Mountain View Village, Mountain View Park, and Residence Park Sofia with signboards mixing Latin-alphabet English and Cyrillic-alphabet Bulgarian.

Suburban housing developers around the world have loved American and Western European branding. Chinese apartment buyers and affluent purchasers of villas can find options with English-language names such as Atlantic Place and a wild mix of styles—Southern Californian, Mediterranean, "European romantic"—that convey prestige and economic success. South African suburbs promise Tuscan delight and Georgian splendor. Affluent families in Bangalore may decide to live in Whispering Pines and Palm Meadows. As new highways opened land on the "good" northern side of Buenos Aires, developers marketed new housing estates for their American lifestyle. "Miamization," named for the US city with the closest ties to South America, describes many of the suburban choices here and in other South American cities. In Jakarta and Bangkok, economically successful families have been flocking to American-style auto-dependent housing estates. These neighborhoods are not clones of Orange County and Las Vegas, but they borrow from their design and marketing toolkits.

This new suburban growth is a product of the new economic regime of the late twentieth and early twenty-first centuries in which government steps back and the private market steps forward. The transition in postsocialist countries has been dramatic. Middle-class Hungarians have sought single-family houses in the northwestern quadrant of the metropolis. Two hundred local governments around Prague have competed to facilitate development of new housing and shopping centers, drawing young and better-educated households to an outer ring. Efforts to meet housing demand in China have created entire forests of high-rise suburbs. Increasing affluence in parts of Latin America have allowed elites to leave older neighbors and central area apartments for new, expensive housing on the suburban frontier. Meanwhile, Parisians with enough euros have been moving to bigger houses in farther-out suburbs and Americans with enough dollars built more than a few McMansions on five-acre parcels—despite the evidence that more compact development is more resource efficient.

The growth of a new upper middle class who have benefited from a growing global economy has also created a demand for gated suburban communities from Southern California to South Africa to South America. Gates and walls are everywhere in new suburban zones. Gates can represent security, and they also signal status. Gated communities in the United States are especially prevalent in the South and Southwest, where suburbs have grown most rapidly in recent decades. The eleven million units in access-secured developments, according to 2015 data, include mobile home parks as well as upscale subdivisions, but it is the latter that are targets for satire. Residents of Arroyo Blanco Estates in T. C. Boyle's *Tortilla Curtain* (1995) fear that their carefully managed subdivision high up Topanga Canyon on the

12. Mountain View Village outside Sofia, Bulgaria, is a gated community that would be at home in the outer suburbs of Denver, Dallas, or Delhi, showing the attraction of the American suburban lifestyle for affluent households around the globe.

west side of Los Angeles is threatened by undocumented Mexican immigrants. It needs a wall, they decide; the workers they hire, ironically, are undocumented. Residents of Heron Bay Estates in John Barth's *The Development* (2008) also think they need a gate as protection from the denizens of Maryland's Eastern Shore, only to blithely leave it open once it is in place.

Gated communities go by different names. They are *urbanizaciones cerradas* in Ecuador and *fraccionamientos cerrados* in Mexico. They are *condomonios fechados* in Brazil, where they have evolved from upper-class privilege to middle-class option. Developers in São Paulo promise walls, iron fences, and gates with twenty-four-hour guards for "permanent tranquility." Hundreds of *barrios privados* have been built on the favored north side of Buenos Aires. Some are *los countries*, country clubs turned into upscale housing estates. Large developments are intended not only to attract residents from older neighborhoods of the metropolis but also to make cities attractive and "safe" for the global elite. Observers have described Ecoville in Curtiba and Piedras Rojas outside Santiago in these terms. Accra counted more than a score of gated suburban estates built or in process in 2004, globalizing the city from the top down. A resident of a gated complex called Nirvana in the vast New Delhi suburb of Gurgaon told an interviewer in 2009 that "I wanted safety and security above everything else…we have like-minded people in Nirvana.…So we understand each other. That's one of the best things Nirvana offers."

The preoccupation with security may have reached an extreme in affluent white suburbs on the north side of Johannesburg. Some homeowners' associations have fortified themselves by erecting gates across public roads to fend off inner-city crime. Other residents can choose among dozens of citadel subdivisions with high walls augmented by razor wire. Their advertising emphasizes security, surveillance, and even armed response teams.

Adapting to new futures

The year 2008 was a bad time to be building out a new subdivision in Florida or California. The collapse of a housing price bubble that was powered by subprime mortgages derailed the American economy and reverberated around the world. Housing markets deflated in Japan, Spain, Austria, and especially the British Isles. The effects were most obvious on the suburban frontier. Journalists, perhaps with a big-city bias, hurried to describe Florida and California subdivisions where half the houses had never been occupied, most of the rest were abandoned, and only one in ten still sheltered a family desperate to save its investment as weeds grew and dust blew. Economic collapse left ghost housing estates scattered around Dublin. Two homicide detectives in Tana French's *Broken Harbor* (2013) enter Ocean

View past a billboard announcing "A New Revelation in Premier Living. Luxury Houses Now Viewing."

> At first glance, Ocean View looked pretty tasty: big detached houses that gave you something substantial for your money, trim strips of green, quaint signposts pointing you toward Little Gems Childcare and Diamondcut Leisure Center. Second glance, the grass needed weeding and there were gaps in the footpaths. Third glance, something was wrong.
>
> The houses were too much alike. Even on the ones where a triumphant red-and-blue sign yelled SOLD, no one had...put flowerpots on the windowsills or tossed plastic kiddie toys on the lawn. There was a scattering of parked cars, but most of the driveways were empty, and not in a way that said that everyone was out powering the economy. You could look straight through three out of four houses.
>
> "Jaysus," Richie said: in the silence his voice was loud enough that both of us jumped. "The village of the damned."

Suburban housing slowly recovered from the Great Recession over the 2010s, but the long crisis is a prompt to think about demographic and environmental limits. Globalized suburbia is about continued growth, but it faces countervailing forces. Italy and Japan now have aging and slowly shrinking populations and other nations are approaching steady-state or declining numbers. Germany has demolished thousands of housing units in its depressed eastern states where numbers are declining. The 2010s recorded the slowest American growth since the 1930s, and the demand for housing now depends as much on immigrant households as on family formation among the native born. Hovering in the background is the challenge of climate change and the necessity to reduce greenhouse gas emissions. Adaptation is about both scaling back and rethinking suburban models, motivated by a quite different context of physically limiting or slowing growth.

Adaptation can be incremental. In the United States, the rise of big-box stores and e-commerce has undercut many older retail malls, making them targets for redevelopment. Mizner Park in Boca Raton, Florida, is one early model, an old mall demolished for new upscale housing and shops; in effect, it is downtown-style redevelopment in an older suburb. More widely useful will be reusing malls and their vast parking lots for affordable infill housing. What about schools built for baby boom suburbs with aging populations? Demolish them, mothball in expectation that immigrant families will provide a new wave of students, or repurpose the buildings for other uses?

In larger context, suburban planning may seem like an afterthought for societies anticipating flooded coastal cities, regional water shortages, devastating heat waves, and tens of millions of climate refugees. It is possible that competition for scarce resources will not only drive richer nations to close their borders but also further polarize suburbs between gated enclaves and shantytowns. That is certainly the scenario in Paolo Bacigalupi's dystopian novel *The Water Knife*, in which Phoenix is split between fortified high-rises and sprawling slums filled with climate refugees from Texas, and the Colorado River is a defended border that protects the privileged arcologies of Las Vegas.

Arcologies are an extreme cure for the environmental impact of suburbs. The wildly visionary architect Paolo Soleri coined the term by combining architecture and ecology. His idea was to replace sprawling cities with vast megastructures where everyone would pile on top of each other while freeing the land of most human intrusions except for necessary agriculture, razing and rewilding suburbia in the process. Frank Lloyd Wright's proposal for Broadacre City was the opposite, dissolving cities by spreading people out on endless expanses of miniature farms. Both schemes make for great conceptual drawings but extremely poor blueprints for action.

Practical incremental changes rather than grand schemes are the best way to mitigate suburban environmental damage. Mature suburbs have been urbanizing for several decades, building mid-rise downtowns as walkable nodes within the metropolitan region; the iconic planned community of Columbia, Maryland, is an example that plans for millions of square feet of new "downtown" space. Interconnecting residential pods and pockets of cul-de-sac subdivisions reduces travel times. Replacing seas of concrete with permeable pavements, narrowing overwide streets, and stacking warehouse floors rather than spreading them horizontally reduce the accumulation of heat. Clustering new development promotes efficient energy use. Transit-oriented development is the American city planning term for surrounding outlying suburban rail stops with apartments—a trendy way to advocate for something that Sweden and Singapore have done for decades. Agricultural reserves, greenbelts, and urban growth boundaries help to keep development focused and compact. In the meanwhile, fend off proposals for extra suburban ring roads and bypasses that are surefire guarantees of more sprawl and will soon be as congested as the highways they claim to supplement.

Suburbs can also be designed in environmentally friendly ways that mitigate heat island effects and contribute to "greening" the landscape. Clustered development can protect natural drainage and watercourses and allocation of open space. Limiting lot sizes to 5,000 square feet—standard for very livable suburbs of the Model T era—reduces driving and allows suburbs to move toward the planning ideal of neighborhoods where basic needs can be satisfied within a walking radius of fifteen minutes. A newly industrialized nation like China, which has experienced breakneck urbanization, will make different choices, but planners for cities like Shanghai are increasingly promoting mid-density, low-energy options that are distant descendants of Garden City ideals. The 2017–50 plan for the wide Melbourne region sets a goal of twenty-minute neighborhoods where essential daily services are less than a kilometer from every resident.

Suburban or postsuburban

Commentators and social scientists sometimes describe the twenty-first century as a "postsuburban" era. Definitions of postsuburbia list varying sets of characteristics: growth that leapfrogs beyond built-up areas and feathers far into the countryside; fragmented landscapes in which housing tucks around industry and commerce; sprawling low-density development without a clear center; and multifocal growth in which a single center is no longer dominant (Los Angeles!) and suburbanites no longer need or use the older city. Thomas Sieverts's coinage of *Zwischenstadt* or "in-between city" to describe the lower-density development reaching between German cities is a European version. Common to postsuburbia is the idea that traditional leafy suburbs for the upper middle class are, at best, survivors in a sea of something new, more varied, and perhaps not as nice.

In fact, the postsuburban characteristics of disconnected development, multiple centers, satellite suburbs, mixing of land uses and social classes, and suburbs as places of production as well as consumption go back such a long way that it is better to avoid the term. Nor have middle-class utopias disappeared—they are behind gates in São Paulo and Johannesburg or around Florida golf courses. Think instead of generations of suburbanization. For more than a century, older suburbs have changed as new suburbs develop. The older suburbs can look "urban" in comparison to newer development, but those newer suburbs mature in turn. We can expect more of the same, with all the fascinating variations on a theme that the outer edges of French, Indonesian, Korean, and Chinese cities will offer.

If suburbs are like peanut butter, twenty-first-century suburbs are the chunky style. North American suburbs were never the uniform single-family landscape of nostalgic memory, but their preferred future is one of edge cities and mid-rise clusters interspersed with traditional subdivisions and threaded green space. The outskirts of Asian and Latin American cities have been converging on the same pattern from different directions. There are many brands of chunky on supermarket shelves, just as the specifics of peripheral development differ from nation to nation, but they are all products and examples of the forces that have given the twenty-first century what we can call an urban–suburban world.

References

Introduction: What is a suburb?

Abrams: Charles Abrams, *The Language of Cities* (New York: Viking Press, 1971), 303.
Weber: Adna Ferrin Weber, *The Growth of Cities in the Nineteenth Century* (New York: Macmillan, 1899), 475.

Chapter 1: The first suburban century

Shakespeare: *Henry VIII*, 5.3.72.
Victorian suburb: H. J. Dyos, *Victorian Suburb: A Study of the Growth of Camberwell* (Leicester, UK: Leicester University Press, 1961), 85.
Lawrence: D. H. Lawrence, *Kangaroo*, ed. Bruce Steele (New York: Cambridge University Press, 1994), 11.
Cinderella suburbs: Graeme Davison, "Suburb Is Not a Dirty Word in Australia," in *What's in a Name: Talking About Urban Peripheries*, ed. Richard Harris and Charlotte Vorms (Toronto: University of Toronto Press, 2017), 78.
Knoxville: James Agee, "Knoxville: Summer of 1915," *Partisan Review* 5 (August–September 1938): 22.
Glendale: James M. Cain, *Mildred Pierce* (1941), in *Cain X 3* (New York: Knopf, 1969), 110.

Chapter 2: Suburbs at flood tide

Knocknaree: Tana French, *In the Woods* (New York: Viking Penguin, 2007), 2.

Rachel Cusk: Rachel Cusk, *Arlington Park* (New York: Picador, 2006), 6, 83.

Ratoath: Mary Corcoran, "God's Golden Acre for Children: Pastoralism and Sense of Place in New Suburban Communities," *Urban Studies* 47, no. 12 (2010): 2546.

Lakewood: D. J. Waldie, *Holy Land: A Suburban Memoir* (New York: W. W. Norton, 2005), Introduction.

Chapter 3: Vertical suburbs

Reputation of *banlieues*: Loic Wacquant, *Urban Outcasts: A Comparative Sociology of Advanced Marginality* (Malden, MA: Polity, 2008), 140.

Chapter 4: Improvised suburbs

Paris in 1922: Nora Evenson, *Paris: A Century of Change, 1878–1978* (New Haven, CT: Yale University Press, 1979), 229.

Chagrin Falls Park: Andrew Wiese, *Places of Their Own: African American Suburbanization in the Twentieth Century* (Chicago: University of Chicago Press, 2004), 74.

Juanita Hammond: Becky Nicolaides, "Where the Workingman Is Welcome: Working Class Suburbs in Los Angeles, 1900–1940," *Pacific Historical Review* 68 (November 1999): 535.

Tortilla Flat: John Steinbeck, *Tortilla Flat* (New York: Modern Library, 1937), 10–11.

Pierre Mac Orlan: Quoted in Christian Topolov, "The Naming Process," in *What's in a Name: Talking About Urban Peripheries*, ed. Richard Harris and Charlotte Vorms (Toronto: University of Toronto Press, 2017), 41.

Colombia National Planning Office: Translated and quoted in Timothy O'Dea Gauhan, "Housing the Urban Poor: The Case of Bogota, Colombia," *Journal of International Studies and World Affairs* 19 (1977): 108.

Chapter 5: Suburban work

Pullman: Richard T. Ely, "Pullman: A Social Study," *Harper's Magazine* 70 (February 1885): 465–66.

Chapter 6: What's wrong with suburbs

Architect 1876: Quoted in F. M. L. Thompson, ed., *The Rise of Suburbia* (Leicester, UK: Leicester University Press, 1982), 3.

Walter Besant: quoted in D. J. Olsen, *The Growth of Victorian London* (New York: Holmes and Meier 1976), 210.

Orwell: George Orwell, *A Clergyman's Daughter* (1935), quoted in Rupa Huq, *Making Sense of Suburbia through Popular Culture* (London: Bloomsbury Academic, 2013), 31; George Orwell, *Coming Up for Air* (London: Gollancz, 1939), chap. 1.

Surbiton: Keble Howard, *The Smiths: A Comedy without a Plot* (New York: McClure, Phillips, 1907), 13, 31.

Palmers Green: Stevie Smith, *Me Again: Uncollected Writings of Stevie Smith*, ed. Jack Barbera and William McBrian (New York: Farrar, Straus and Giroux, 1982), 100–104.

Catherine Bauer: *Architectural Forum*, 105 (September 1956): 103.

William Whyte: William H. Whyte Jr., "A Plan to Save Vanishing U.S. Countryside," *Life* 47, no. 7 (August 19, 1959): 88–89.

Kadohata: Cynthia Kadohata, *In the Heart of the Valley of Love* (New York: Viking, 1992), 2, 33, 124.

Compton: Richard Elman, *Ill-at-Ease in Compton* (New York: Pantheon, 1967), 4.

Coupland: Douglas Coupland, *Generation X* (New York: St. Martin's, 1991), 14–15.

Chapter 7: Two hundred years and counting

Gurgaon: Sarah Goodyear, "The Threat of Gated Communities," Bloomberg CityLab, July 15, 2013, https://www.bloomberg.com/news/articles/2013-07-15/the-threat-of-gated-communities.

Broken Harbor: Tana French, *Broken Harbor* (New York: Viking Penguin, 2012), 13.

Further reading

Global surveys

Berger, Alan M., Joel Kotkin, and Celina Balderas Guzmán, eds. *Infinite Suburbia*. Hudson, NY: Princeton Architectural Press, 2017.

Hanlon, Bernadette, and Thomas Vicino, eds. *Routledge Companion to the Suburbs*. Abingdon, UK: Routledge, 2019.

Harris, Richard. *The Suburban Land Question: A Global Survey*. Toronto: University of Toronto Press, 2018.

Harris, Richard, and Charlotte Vorms. *What's in a Name: Talking About Urban Peripheries*. Toronto: University of Toronto Press, 2017.

Keil, Roger. *Suburban Planet: Making the World Suburban from the Outside In*. Medford, MA: Polity Press, 2018.

Kwak, Nancy, and Andrew Sandoval-Strauss. *Making Cities Global*. Philadelphia: University of Pennsylvania Press, 2017.

Phelps, Nicholas, and Fulong Wu. *International Perspectives on Suburbanization: A Post-suburban World?* New York: Palgrave Macmillan, 2011.

Stanilov, Kiril, and Brenda Case Scheer. *Suburban Form: An International Perspective*. Abingdon, UK: Routledge, 2003.

Tutino, John, and Martin Melosi, eds. *New World Cities: Challenges of Urbanization and Globalization in the Americas*. Chapel Hill: University of North Carolina Press, 2019.

Improvised suburbs

Gilbert, Alan. *Cities, Poverty and Development: Urbanization in the Third World*. New York: Oxford University Press, 1992.

Harris, Richard. *Unplanned Suburbs: Toronto's American Tragedy, 1900–1950*. Baltimore: Johns Hopkins University Press, 1996.

Kwak, Nancy. *A World of Homeowners: American Power and the Politics of Housing Aid*. Chicago: University of Chicago Press, 2015.

McCann, Bryan. *Hard Times in the Marvelous City: From Dictatorship to Democracy in the Favelas of Rio de Janeiro*. Durham, NC: Duke University Press, 2014.

Neuwarth, Robert. *Shadow Cities: A Billion Squatters, a New Urban World*. New York: Routledge, 2004.

Nicolaides, Becky. *My Blue Heaven: Life and Politics in the Working-Class Suburbs of Los Angeles, 1920–1965*. Chicago: University of Chicago Press, 2002.

Perlman, Janice. *Favela: Four Decades of Living on the Edge in Rio de Janeiro*. New York: Oxford University Press, 2010.

New towns

Arnold, Joseph. *The New Deal in the Suburbs: A History of the Greenbelt Town Program, 1935–54*. Columbus: Ohio State University Press, 1971.

Bloom, Nicholas Dagen. *Suburban Alchemy: 1960s New Towns and the Transformation of the American Dream*. Columbus: Ohio State University Press, 2001.

Forsyth, Ann. *Reforming Suburbia: The Planned Communities of Irvine, Columbia and the Woodlands*. Berkeley: University of California Press, 2005.

Peiser, Richard, and Ann Forsyth, eds. *New Towns for the Twenty-First Century: A Guide to Planned Communities Worldwide*. Philadelphia: University of Pennsylvania Press, 2021.

Sies, Mary, Isabelle Gournay, and Rob Freestone, eds. *Iconic Planned Communities and the Challenge of Change*. Philadelphia: University of Pennsylvania Press, 2019.

Wakeman, Rosemary. *Practicing Utopia: An Intellectual History of the New Town Movement*. Chicago: University of Chicago Press, 2016.

Politics and inequality

Glotzer, Paige, *How the Suburbs Were Segregated: Developers and the Business of Exclusionary Housing, 1890–1960*. New York: Columbia University Press, 2020.

Kneebone, Elizabeth, and Alan Berube. *Confronting Suburban Poverty in America*. Washington, DC: Brookings Institution Press, 2014.

Lassiter, Matthew. *The Silent Majority: Suburban Politics in the Sunbelt South*. Princeton, NJ: Princeton University Press, 2007.

Lung-Amam, Willow. *Trespassers? Asian Americans and the Battle for Suburbia*. Berkeley: University of California Press, 2017.

McGirr, Lisa. *Suburban Warriors: The Origins of the New American Right*. Princeton, NJ: Princeton University Press, 2015.

Orfield, Myron. *American Metropolitics: The New Suburban Reality*. Washington, DC: Brookings Institution, 2002.

Self, Robert. *American Babylon: Race and the Struggle for Postwar Oakland*. Princeton, NJ: Princeton University Press. 2005.

Vicino, Thomas. *Transforming Race and Class in Suburbia: Decline in Metropolitan Baltimore*. New York: Palgrave Macmillan, 2008.

Wacquant, Loic. *Urban Outcasts: A Comparative Sociology of Advanced Marginality*. Malden, MA: Polity, 2008.

Wiese, Andrew. *Places of Their Own: African American Suburbanization in the Twentieth Century*. Chicago: University of Chicago Press, 2004.

Sociology classics

Berger, Bennett. *Working Class Suburb: A Study of Autoworkers in Suburbia*. Berkeley: University of California Press, 1960.

Clark, S. D. *The Suburban Society*. Toronto: University of Toronto Press, 1966.

Douglas, Harlan P. *The Suburban Trend*. New York: Century, 1925.

Gans, Herbert. *The Levittowners: Ways of Life and Politics in a New Suburban Community*. New York: Pantheon, 1967.

Whyte, William H. *The Organization Man*. New York: Simon & Schuster, 1956.

Young, Michael, and Peter Willmott. *Family and Kinship in East London*. London: Routledge & Kegan Paul, 1957.

Suburban economies

Garreau, Joel. *Edge City: Life on the New Frontier*. New York: Doubleday, 1991.

Hise, Greg. *Magnetic Los Angeles*: Baltimore: Johns Hopkins University Press, 1997.

Lang, Robert. *Edgeless Cities: Exploring the Elusive Metropolis.* Washington, DC: Brookings Institute, 2003.

Lewis, Robert, ed. *Manufacturing Suburbs: Building Work and Home on the Metropolitan Fringe.* Philadelphia: Temple University Press, 2004.

Murray, Martin J. *City of Extremes: The Spatial Politics of Johannesburg.* Durham, NC: Duke University Press, 2011.

O'Mara, Margaret. *Cities of Knowledge: Cold War Science and the Search for the Next Silicon Valley.* Princeton, NJ: Princeton University Press, 2005.

Suburban reputation

Bilson, Sarah. *The Promise of the Suburbs: A Victorian History in Literature and Culture.* New Haven, CT: Yale University Press, 2019.

Bruegmann, Robert. *Sprawl: A Compact History.* Chicago: University of Chicago Press, 2005.

Clapson, Mark. *Suburban Century: Social Change and Growth in England and the USA.* London: Bloomsbury, 2003.

Donaldson, Scott. *The Suburban Myth.* New York: Columbia University Press, 1969.

Huq, Rupa. *Making Sense of Suburbia through Popular Culture.* London: Bloomsbury, 2013.

Anglo-American suburbs

Barraclough, Laura. *Making the San Fernando Valley: Rural Landscapes, Urban Development and White Privilege.* Athens, GA: University of Georgia Press, 2011.

Baxandall, Rosalyn, and Elizabeth Ewen. *Picture Windows: How the Suburbs Happened.* New York: Basic Books, 2000.

Cohen, Lizabeth. *A Consumer's Republic: The Politics of Mass Consumption in Postwar America.* New York: Knopf, 2003.

Dyos, H. J. *Victorian Suburb: A Study of the Growth of Camberwell.* Leicester, UK: Leicester University Press, 1961.

Fishman, Robert. *Bourgeois Utopias: The Rise and Fall of Suburbia.* New York: Basic Books, 1987.

Gutfreund, Owen. *Twentieth Century Sprawl: Highways and the Reshaping of the American Landscape.* New York: Oxford University Press, 2007.

Harris, Richard. *Creeping Conformity: How Canada Became Suburban, 1900–1960*. Toronto: University of Toronto Press, 2014.

Hayden, Dolores. *Building Suburbia: Green Fields and Urban Growth, 1820–2000*. New York: Pantheon, 2003.

Jackson, Kenneth T. *Crabgrass Frontier*. New York: Oxford University Press, 1985.

Kelly, Barbara. *Expanding the American Dream: Building and Rebuilding Levittown*. Albany: State University of New York Press, 1993.

Mace, Alan. *City Suburbs: Placing Suburbs in a Post-suburban World*. Abingdon, UK: Routledge, 2013.

Teaford, Jon C. *City and Suburb: The Political Fragmentation of Metropolitan America, 1850–1970*. Baltimore: Johns Hopkins University Press, 1979.

Warner, Sam Bass, Jr. *Streetcar Suburbs: The Process of Growth in Boston 1870–1900*. Cambridge, MA: Harvard University Press, 1962.

China

Campanella, Thomas. *The Concrete Dragon*. New York: Princeton Architectural Press, 2011.

Fleischer, Frederike. *Suburban Beijing: Housing and Consumption in Contemporary China*. Minneapolis: University of Minnesota Press, 2010.

Hsing, You-Tien. *The Great Urban Transformation: Politics of Land and Property in China*. New York: Oxford University Press, 2010.

Wu, Fulong. *Planning for Growth: Urban and Regional Planning in China*. Abingdon, UK: Routledge, 2015.

Eastern Europe

Hirt, Sonia. *Iron Curtains: Gates, Suburbs and Privatization of Space in the Post-socialist City*. Oxford: Wiley–Blackwell, 2012.

Stanilov, Kiril. *The Post-socialist City: Urban Form and Space Transformations in Central and Eastern Europe after Socialism*. Dordrecht, The Netherlands: Springer, 2007.

Stanilov, Kiril, and Ludek Sykora, eds. *Confronting Suburbanization: Urban Decentralization in Postsocialist Central and Eastern Europe*. Oxford: Wiley–Blackwell, 2014.

Suburbs

Index

Index

Suburbs